Grade 5

Pearson Scott Foresman

Leveled Reader
Teaching Guide

Glenview, Illinois • Boston, Massachusetts • Chandler, Arizona • Upper Saddle River, New Jersey

Accelerated Reader®

ISBN: 13: 978-0-328-48456-0
ISBN: 10: 0-328-48456-3
10 V016 15 14 13

Table of Contents

Introduction. **4**

Measure Fluent Reading **6**

Observation Checklist **8**

About My Reading. **9**

Reading Strategy Assessment. **10**

Progress Report. **11**

LEVELED READER TITLE	Instruction	Comprehension Practice	Vocabulary Practice
The Signs	12–13	14	15
Weather Forecasting	16–17	18	19
The Medicine Harvest	20–21	22	23
The Journey of African American Athletes	24–25	26	27
The Land of Opportunity	28–29	30	31
Our Essential Oceans	32–33	34	35
The Most Dangerous Woman in America	36–37	38	39
Moving to Mali	40–41	42	43
The Talker	44–45	46	47
The National Guard: Today's Minutemen	48–49	50	51
Philo and His Invention	52–53	54	55
Art's Inspiration	56–57	58	59
What's New with Dinosaur Fossils?	60–61	62	63
The Blues Evolution	64–65	66	67
Special Effects in Hollywood	68–69	70	71
Cheaper, Faster, and Better	72–73	74	75
Operation Inspiration	76–77	78	79

LEVELED READER TITLE	Instruction	Comprehension Practice	Vocabulary Practice
Can Humans Make a Home in Outer Space?	80–81	82	83
Nathaniel Comes to Town	84–85	86	87
What Makes Great Athletes?	88–89	90	91
The Sandwich Brigade	92–93	94	95
Space Travel Inventions	96–97	98	99
Astronauts and Cosmonauts	100–101	102	103
The Shaping of the Continents	104–105	106	107
From Territory to Statehood	108–109	110	111
How the Wolves Saved Yellowstone	112–113	114	115
Mixed-Up Vegetables	116–117	118	119
Precious Goods: From Salt to Silk	120–121	122	123
Traveling by Plane	124–125	126	127
Unexpected Music	128–129	130	131

Graphic Organizers

Story Prediction from Previewing **132**

Story Prediction from Vocabulary **133**

KWL Chart **134**

Vocabulary Frame **135**

Story Sequence A **136**

Story Sequence B **137**

Story Elements **138**

Question the Author **139**

Plot Structure **140**

Story Comparison **141**

Web **142**

Main Idea **143**

Venn Diagram **144**

Compare and Contrast **145**

Cause and Effect **146**

Problem and Solution **147**

Time Line **148**

Steps in a Process **149**

Three-Column Chart **150**

Four-Column Chart **151**

Five-Column Chart **152**

Answer Key **153**

Introduction

Scott Foresman *Reading Street* provides more than 750 leveled readers that help students become better readers and build a lifelong love of reading. The *Reading Street* leveled readers are engaging texts that help students practice critical reading skills and strategies. They also provide opportunities to build vocabulary, understand concepts, and develop reading fluency.

The leveled readers were developed to be age-appropriate and appealing to students at each grade level. The leveled readers consist of engaging texts in a variety of genres, including fantasy, folk tales, realistic fiction, historical fiction, and narrative and expository nonfiction. To better address real-life reading skills that students will encounter in testing situations and beyond, a higher percentage of nonfiction texts is provided at each grade.

USING THE LEVELED READERS

You can use the leveled readers to meet the diverse needs of your students. Consider using the readers to

- practice critical skills and strategies
- build fluency
- build vocabulary and concepts
- build background for the main selections in the student book
- provide a variety of reading experiences, e.g., shared, group, individual, take-home, readers' theater

GUIDED READING APPROACH

The *Reading Street* leveled readers are leveled according to Guided Reading criteria by experts trained in Guided Reading. The Guided Reading levels increase in difficulty within a grade level and across grade levels. In addition to leveling according to Guided Reading criteria, the instruction provided in the *Leveled Reader Teaching Guide* is compatible with Guided Reading instruction. An instructional routine is provided for each leveled reader. This routine is most effective when working with individual students or small groups.

MANAGING THE CLASSROOM

When using the leveled readers with individuals or small groups, you'll want to keep the other students engaged in meaningful, independent learning tasks. Establishing independent practice stations throughout the classroom and routines for these stations can help you manage the rest of the class while you work with individuals or small groups. Practice stations can include listening, phonics, vocabulary, independent reading, and cross-curricular activities. For classroom management, create a work board that lists the stations and which students should be at each station. Provide instructions at each station that detail the tasks to be accomplished. Update the board and alert students when they should rotate to a new station. For additional support for managing your classroom, see the *Reading Street* Practice Stations' *Classroom Management Handbook.*

USING THE LEVELED READER TEACHING GUIDE

The *Leveled Reader Teaching Guide* provides an instruction plan for each leveled reader based on the same instructional routine.

INTRODUCE THE BOOK The Introduction includes suggestions for creating interest in the text by discussing the title and author, building background, and previewing the book and its features.

READ THE BOOK Before students begin reading the book, have them set purposes for reading and discuss how they can use the reading strategy as they read. Determine how you want students in a particular group to read the text, softly or silently, to a specific point or the entire text. Then use the Comprehension Questions to provide support as needed and to assess comprehension.

REVISIT THE BOOK The Reader Response questions provide opportunities for students to demonstrate their understanding of the text, the target comprehension skill, and vocabulary. The Response Options require students to revisit the text to respond to what they've read and to move beyond the text to explore related content.

SKILL WORK The Skill Work box provides instruction and practice for the target skill and strategy and selection vocabulary. Instruction for an alternate comprehension skill allows teachers to provide additional skill instruction and practice for students.

USING THE GRAPHIC ORGANIZERS

Graphic organizers in blackline-master format can be found on pages 132–152. These can be used as overhead transparencies or as student worksheets.

ASSESSING PERFORMANCE

Use the assessment forms that begin on page 6 to make notes about your students' reading skills, use of reading strategies, and general reading behaviors.

MEASURE FLUENT READING (pp. 6–7) Provides directions for measuring a student's fluency, based on words correct per minute (wcpm), and reading accuracy using a running record.

OBSERVATION CHECKLIST (p. 8) Allows you to note the regularity with which students demonstrate their understanding and use of reading skills and strategies.

STUDENT SELF-ASSESSMENT (p. 9) Helps students identify their own areas of strength and areas where they need further work. This form (About My Reading) encourages them to list steps they can take to become better readers and to set goals as readers. Suggest that students share their self-assessment notes with their families so that family members can work with them more effectively to practice their reading skills and strategies at home.

READING STRATEGY ASSESSMENT (p. 10) Provides criteria for evaluating each student's proficiency as a strategic reader.

PROGRESS REPORT (p. 11) Provides a means to track a student's book-reading progress over a period of time by noting the level at which a student reads and his or her accuracy at that level. Reading the chart from left to right gives you a visual model of how quickly a student is making the transition from one level to the next. Share these reports with parents or guardians to help them see how their child's reading is progressing.

Measure
Fluent Reading

Taking a Running Record

A running record is an assessment of a student's oral reading accuracy and oral reading fluency. Reading accuracy is based on the number of words read correctly. Reading fluency is based on the reading rate (the number of words correct per minute) and the degree to which a student reads with a "natural flow."

How to Measure Reading Accuracy

1. Choose a grade-level text of about 80 to 120 words that is unfamiliar to the student.
2. Make a copy of the text for yourself. Make a copy for the student or have the student read aloud from a book.
3. Give the student the text and have the student read aloud. (You may wish to record the student's reading for later evaluation.)
4. On your copy of the text, mark any miscues or errors the student makes while reading. See the running record sample on page 7, which shows how to identify and mark miscues.
5. Count the total number of words in the text and the total number of errors made by the student. Note: If a student makes the same error more than once, such as mispronouncing the same word multiple times, count it as one error. Self-corrections do not count as actual errors. Use the following formula to calculate the percentage score, or accuracy rate:

$$\frac{\text{Total Number of Words} - \text{Total Number of Errors}}{\text{Total Number of Words}} \times 100 = \text{percentage score}$$

Interpreting the Results

- A student who reads **95–100%** of the words correctly is reading at an **independent level** and may need more challenging text.
- A student who reads **90–94%** of the words correctly is reading at an **instructional level** and will likely benefit from guided instruction.
- A student who reads **89%** or fewer of the words correctly is reading at a **frustrational level** and may benefit most from targeted instruction with lower-level texts and intervention.

How to Measure Reading Rate (WCPM)

1. Follow Steps 1–3 above.
2. Note the exact times when the student begins and finishes reading.
3. Use the following formula to calculate the number of words correct per minute (WCPM):

$$\frac{\text{Total Number of Words Read Correctly}}{\text{Total Number of Seconds}} \times 60 = \text{words correct per minute}$$

Interpreting the Results

By the end of the year, a fifth-grader should be reading approximately 130–140 WCPM.

Running Record Sample

Running Record Sample

Notations

Did you know that every day in   **7**
cities across the United States, students   **13**
just like you are helping others?   **19**

    Each year in <u>Louisiana</u>, a young   **25** (H.)
student and her younger brother have   **31**
gone around collecting stuffed animals   **36**
for children who live in a homeless   **43** (the)
shelter.   **44**

    In New York City, seventy-six   **49**
students from Harlem teamed up with   **55**
four Olympic athletes to transform   **60**
a run-down park into a playground   **66**
featuring a daffodil garden.   **70**

    And ~~each~~ year in Indiana, a young   **77** (every)
student has gone around collecting   **82**
hundreds of bundles of baby clothes   **88** (SC)
and other baby items. In the fall she   **96**
delivers them to a home for mothers   **103**
who are having tough times.   **108** /tug/

Accurate Reading
The student reads a word correctly.

Hesitation
The student hesitates over a word, and the teacher provides the word. Wait several seconds before telling the student what the word is.

Insertion
The student inserts words or parts of words that are not in the text.

Omission
The student omits words or word parts.

Substitution
The student substitutes words or parts of words for the words in the text.

Self-correction
The student reads a word incorrectly but then corrects the error. Do not count self-corrections as actual errors. However, noting self-corrections will help you identify words the student finds difficult.

Mispronunciation/Misreading
The student pronounces or reads a word incorrectly.

Running Record Results
Total Number of Words: **108**
Number of Errors: **5**

Reading Time: **51 seconds**

▶ **Reading Accuracy**
$$\frac{108 - 5}{108} \times 100 = 95.370 = 95\%$$

Accuracy Percentage Score: **95%**

▶ **Reading Rate—WCPM**
$$\frac{103}{51} \times 60 = 121.18 = 121 \text{ words correct per minute}$$

Reading Rate: **121 WCPM**

Observation Checklist

Student's Name_____ Date _____

Behaviors Observed	Always (Proficient)	Usually (Fluent)	Sometimes (Developing)	Rarely (Novice)

Reading Strategies and Skills

Behaviors Observed	Always (Proficient)	Usually (Fluent)	Sometimes (Developing)	Rarely (Novice)
Uses prior knowledge and preview to understand what book is about				
Makes predictions and checks them while reading				
Uses context clues to figure out meanings of new words				
Uses phonics and syllabication to decode words				
Self-corrects while reading				
Reads at an appropriate reading rate				
Reads with appropriate intonation and stress				
Uses fix-up strategies				
Identifies story elements: character, setting, plot, theme				
Summarizes plot or main ideas accurately				
Uses target comprehension skill to understand the text better				
Responds thoughtfully about the text				

Reading Behaviors and Attitudes

Enjoys listening to stories				
Chooses reading as a free-time activity				
Reads with sustained interest and attention				
Participates in discussion about books				

General Comments

About My Reading

Name _____ Date _____

1. Compared with earlier in the year, I am enjoying reading

   ☐ more   ☐ less   ☐ about the same

2. When I read now, I understand

   ☐ more than I used to   ☐ about the same as I used to

3. One thing that has helped me with my reading is

   _____

   _____

   _____

4. One thing that could make me a better reader is

   _____

   _____

   _____

5. Here is one selection or book that I really enjoyed reading:

   _____

   _____

6. Here are some reasons why I liked it:

   _____

   _____

   _____

   _____

   _____

   _____

Reading Strategy Assessment

Student _____   Date _____

Teacher _____

		Proficient	Developing	Emerging	Not showing trait
Building Background Comments:	Previews	☐	☐	☐	☐
	Asks questions	☐	☐	☐	☐
	Predicts	☐	☐	☐	☐
	Activates prior knowledge	☐	☐	☐	☐
	Sets own purposes for reading	☐	☐	☐	☐
	Other:	☐	☐	☐	☐
Comprehension Comments:	Retells/summarizes	☐	☐	☐	☐
	Questions, evaluates ideas	☐	☐	☐	☐
	Relates to self/other texts	☐	☐	☐	☐
	Paraphrases	☐	☐	☐	☐
	Rereads/reads ahead for meaning	☐	☐	☐	☐
	Visualizes	☐	☐	☐	☐
	Uses decoding strategies	☐	☐	☐	☐
	Uses vocabulary strategies	☐	☐	☐	☐
	Understands key ideas of a text	☐	☐	☐	☐
	Other:	☐	☐	☐	☐
Fluency Comments:	Adjusts reading rate	☐	☐	☐	☐
	Reads for accuracy	☐	☐	☐	☐
	Uses expression	☐	☐	☐	☐
	Other:	☐	☐	☐	☐
Connections Comments:	Relates text to self	☐	☐	☐	☐
	Relates text to text	☐	☐	☐	☐
	Relates text to world	☐	☐	☐	☐
	Other:	☐	☐	☐	☐
Self-Assessment Comments:	Is aware of: Strengths	☐	☐	☐	☐
	Needs	☐	☐	☐	☐
	Improvement/achievement	☐	☐	☐	☐
	Sets and implements learning goals	☐	☐	☐	☐
	Maintains logs, records, portfolio	☐	☐	☐	☐
	Works with others	☐	☐	☐	☐
	Shares ideas and materials	☐	☐	☐	☐
	Other:	☐	☐	☐	☐

Progress Report

Student's Name _____

At the top of the chart, record the book title, its grade/unit/week (for example, 1.2.3), and the student's accuracy percentage. See page 6 for measuring fluency, calculating accuracy and reading rates. At the bottom of the chart, record the date you took the running record. In the middle of the chart, make an X in the box across from the level of the student's reading—frustrational level (below 89% accuracy), instructional level (90–94% accuracy), or independent level (95–100% accuracy). Record the reading rate (WCPM) in the next row.

Book Title						
Grade/Unit/Week						
Reading Accuracy Percentage						
LEVEL **Frustrational** (89% or below)						
Instructional (90–94%)						
Independent (95% or above)						
Reading Rate (WCPM)						
Date						

The Signs

SUMMARY In this story, Nathan and his mother visit Nathan's grandfather at the Gila River Indian Community in Arizona. In fact, Nathan and his mother are contemplating a move to Arizona from New York City. Nathan wants to support his mother but isn't sure he's ready to give up big city life for this quiet community—that is, until a walk in the wilderness with his grandfather helps him make a decision.

LESSON VOCABULARY

amid	butte
cluttered	exertion
hindsight	input
metaphor	notion
progressed	

INTRODUCE THE BOOK

INTRODUCE THE TITLE AND AUTHOR Discuss with students the title and author of *The Signs*. Ask students to tell what they think this book will be about based on the title and cover illustration.

BUILD BACKGROUND Invite students to participate in a discussion about the members of their family or friends who are important to them. Ask students to think about how they might help these people if they became sick or injured. Share with students a time when trusting your instincts in a situation turned out to be the right thing to do.

PREVIEW/USE TEXT FEATURES Have students preview the book by looking at the illustrations. Ask students to discuss how these text features give an idea of what the book will be about. Ask students what clues the illustrations give to what Nathan will need to do in this story.

READ THE BOOK

SET PURPOSE Have students set a purpose for reading *The Signs*. The engaging illustrations in this story should help to guide this purpose.

STRATEGY SUPPORT: MONITOR AND CLARIFY Have students take notes as they read and then instruct them to prepare an outline of *The Signs*. Remind students that an outline can help them better understand how a piece of writing is organized and can serve as a way of summarizing text to support comprehension. After each student has completed an outline, have students work in small groups to share outline details and to come up with a final outline to share with the class. Use these discussions as an opportunity to review concepts, such as the conflict and theme of the story.

COMPREHENSION QUESTIONS

PAGE 4 Why was Nathan hesitant to move back to Gila River? *(Nathan thought he would miss his life in New York City—the street noise, subway rides, sidewalk street-vendor snacks, and after-school hoops at the Y.)*

PAGE 5 What clue does the author give to let you know something might happen to Nathan's grandfather? *(The author tells us that although it was cool in the kitchen, there were beads of sweat on Grandfather's forehead.)*

PAGE 13 What were Nathan's first thoughts as he ran to find help for his grandfather? *(Nathan had no idea how he was going to find the shortcut his grandfather mentioned. He couldn't even remember how to go back the way they had come.)*

PAGES 15–16 What experiences did Nathan have that proved his grandfather was right when he said "You have walked this way before, and your feet do not forget"? *(Nathan pictured a butte with a Pima hut in front of it—then he saw the butte. Later, he pictured a cottonwood tree beneath a cliff and then saw the tree.)*

REVISIT THE BOOK

READER RESPONSE

1. Possible response: He acts partly on instinct and partly on things he remembers from when he was little. He learns he isn't just a city kid. He is also a Pima Indian who can learn more about himself by living at Gila River.
2. Responses will vary but should reflect evidence of self-monitoring.
3. Possible response: *Hindsight* means, "ability to see, after the event is over, what should have been done." Clues include that *sight* means "power of seeing" and *hind* means "back."
4. Responses will vary.

EXTEND UNDERSTANDING Have students review the illustrations in this selection. Ask them how the illustrations on pages 14, 17, 18, 19, and 20 help them better understand what Nathan went through to help his grandfather.

RESPONSE OPTIONS

WRITING Ask children to imagine that they are Nathan and challenge them to summarize Nathan's adventure in a journal entry. Tell them to be sure to include details from the story in their journal entries.

ELL Explain to students that in this story Nathan discovers how proud he is of his Indian heritage. Invite students to share the things about their own cultures that make them proud.

SOCIAL STUDIES CONNECTION

Time For SOCIAL STUDIES

Students can use the library or the Internet to learn more about The Gila River Indian Community and the Maricopa and Pima tribes. Have students prepare an oral presentation on what they learn and present it to the class.

Skill Work

TEACH/REVIEW VOCABULARY

To help students understand the meaning of *butte*, have them read the second paragraph on page 7. Ask: What words help you understand the meaning of *butte*? Repeat this exercise with other vocabulary words.

TARGET SKILL AND STRATEGY

CHARACTER AND PLOT Remind students that a *character* is a person who takes part in the events of a story. Challenge students, as they read, to look for clues—such as words and actions—that reveal what characters are like. Remind them that the *plot* is an organized sequence of events. Authors use flashbacks to talk about events from the past and foreshadowing to hint at events to come. Invite them to find flashbacks and foreshadowing in the plot.

MONITOR AND CLARIFY Encourage students to develop a reading plan. Note that there are likely to be new words and challenging concepts in the text, so students will want to adopt *monitoring* strategies to checking their comprehension as they read. Encourage students to use *clarifying* strategies when they find they are not comprehending the text: summarizing events to clarify ideas and pinpoint causes and effects; using the context clues surrounding confusing text; rereading sections of text; using illustrations to clarify understanding.

ADDITIONAL SKILL INSTRUCTION

AUTHOR'S PURPOSE Remind students that an *author's purpose* can be to inform, to persuade, to entertain, or to express feelings. Based on their previews, ask students what they think the author's purpose is for *Signs*. Revisit their answers after students have finished reading the book. Do they want to change their opinion about the author's purpose? Why or why not?

Character and Plot

- A **character** is a person who takes part in the events of a story.
- The **plot** is an organized sequence of events. Authors often use flashbacks to tell about something that has already happened and foreshadowing to hint at events to come.

Directions Fill in the graphic organizer below. Under Events, include flashbacks and foreshadowing.

Title _____

Characters

Setting

Problem

Events

_____
_____
_____
_____
_____
_____
_____

Solution

Vocabulary

Directions Draw a line from each word to its definition.

Check the Words You Know

___amid   ___butte   ___cluttered
___exertion   ___hindsight   ___input
___metaphor   ___notion   ___progressed

1. amid   **a.** littered with things

2. butte   **b.** someone's comments or opinions

3. cluttered   **c.** moved forward or ahead

4. exertion   **d.** surrounded by; among

5. hindsight   **e.** opinion, belief

6. input   **f.** steep hill with a flat top

7. metaphor   **g.** use of great effort

8. notion   **h.** ability to see what should have been done

9. progressed   **i.** comparing one thing to something else

Directions Choose three words from the box and write a sentence for each.

10. _____

_____

11. _____

_____

12. _____

_____

Weather Forecasting

SUMMARY This book notes the vital role that weather plays in our lives and the challenges that exist in predicting weather accurately. The book also describes the role of meteorologists and the tools, both conventional and high-tech, that they use to forecast weather on land, at sea, and in the air.

LESSON VOCABULARY

anemometer	atmosphere
barometer	Doppler radar
hygrometer	meteorologists
radiosondes	troposphere
weather forecasts	

INTRODUCE THE BOOK

INTRODUCE THE TITLE AND AUTHOR Discuss with students the title and the author of *Weather Forecasting*. Have students discuss why being able to forecast the weather is important.

BUILD BACKGROUND Have students discuss ways in which they and family members use weather forecasts in their daily lives. Ask: Where do you find weather forecasts? How has recent weather affected your weekend or vacation plans? Has a sudden weather change ever caught you off-guard?

PREVIEW/USE TEXT FEATURES Have students preview the book by looking at the photographs. Then have students look at the diagram and explanation on pages 6–7 on the layers in the atmosphere and the time-lapse photo on page 17 that tracks the path of Hurricane Andrew. Ask: What do you think you will learn from this book?

READ THE BOOK

SET PURPOSE Ask students to set a purpose for reading *Weather Forecasting*. Ideas might include: to learn about weather tools, to learn how meteorologists forecast the weather, and to understand the movement of storms.

STRATEGY SUPPORT: SUMMARIZE Remind students that to *summarize* means to briefly tell what happened in a story. Have students review the main ideas in the book that they wrote down. Ask them to write a short summary of the entire book, based on their notes of the most important parts.

COMPREHENSION QUESTIONS

PAGE 4 From the chart, which days in the 10-day forecast show a low temperature of 54 degrees or higher? *(Friday, Saturday, Sunday, and Monday)*

PAGE 13 Why would a meteorologist use a hygrometer? *(to measure humidity)*

PAGE 13 What causes the cups to spin faster in an anemometer? *(increases in wind speeds)*

PAGES 16 AND 18 How are a radiosonde and dropwindsonde related? *(A dropwindsonde is a type of radiosonde, which is a balloon data-retrieval device. It captures data about atmospheric conditions and relays it to a weather airplane.)*

PAGE 21 How are the two weather maps different? *(Top map shows a temperature forecast; bottom shows a weather forecast.)*

REVISIT THE BOOK

READER RESPONSE

1. The sun heats the atmosphere, which sets air in motion.

2. Responses will vary but should be main ideas from the book. Summary should also be generalizations on how people forecast the weather.

3. *Doppler effect.* Possible response: The Doppler effect made the car's siren sound different in different places.

4. Answers will vary. Students might have been helped by seeing the various objects in different layers.

EXTEND UNDERSTANDING Tell students that many people say weather forecasting is part science, part art. Have students discuss this.

ELL Tell students that there are nonscientific ways that people predict impending weather conditions. For example, some people say that if their knee aches, rain is on the way. Encourage students to tell similar common sayings they know.

RESPONSE OPTIONS

SPEAKING Bring in a copy of a local newspaper. Have students prepare and present short weather forecasts for the next two days, based on information on the weather page.

SCIENCE CONNECTION

Have students research the differences between the causes and effects of tornadoes and hurricanes.

Skill Work

TEACH/REVIEW VOCABULARY

Write the vocabulary words on the board. Ask students to give the definitions of any vocabulary words they know. Have them identify parts of words that give clues (suffix *-ist* in *meteorologist* indicates this word refers to someone who specializes in something, or *meter* in *barometer* may indicate something that measures, as in *thermometer*). Have students look up unfamiliar words in the Glossary.

TARGET SKILL AND STRATEGY

CAUSE AND EFFECT Remind students that a *cause* is why something happened; an *effect* is what happened. Note that sometimes a cause may have multiple effects and an effect may have more than one cause. Remind students that sometimes clue words like *because* and *so* will help establish cause and effect. As they read about forecasting weather, encourage students to ask themselves: What causes this to happen?

SUMMARIZE Remind students that to *summarize* means to briefly tell what happened in a book. Have students list the main ideas in the story as they read.

ADDITIONAL SKILL INSTRUCTION

AUTHOR'S PURPOSE Remind students that an *author's purpose* is the reason he or she has for writing and that often writers have more than one purpose. There are four main purposes: to persuade, to inform, to entertain, and to express. Ask: What do you think the author's purpose is in writing *Weather Forecasting*? Encourage students to continue to examine the author's purpose as they read.

Cause and Effect

- A **cause** is the reason something happens. The **effect** is what happens.
- A cause may have more than one effect, and an effect may have more than one cause.
- Sometimes a cause is not directly stated. You need to think about why something happened.

Directions Read the following passage. Then answer the questions that follow.

> Hurricanes are huge tropical storms. The warm humid air of the tropics rises. As the air rises, it cools, and the moisture condenses to cloud and rain drops. Heat energy is released in this condensation process. In addition, winds collide and push warm, moist air upward. This rising air reinforces the air that is already rising from the surface, so the circulation and wind speeds of the storm increase. A tropical storm with a wind speed of 74 miles per hour is classified as a hurricane. When a hurricane makes landfall it loses the tropical moisture and weakens rapidly. But it can cause massive damage before it does.
>
> High winds are a primary cause of the loss of life and home destruction that can result from hurricanes. Winds create airborne projectiles out of trees and sharp objects that hurl through the air and then bang into homes, businesses, and even people. In addition, flooding caused by the coastal storm surge of the ocean and the massive rains that come with hurricanes create damage. Hurricanes have destroyed fishing piers and other businesses too.

1. What are two major causes of hurricanes?

_____

_____

2. Name two major causes of hurricane damage.

_____

_____

3. What is one major effect of hurricanes?

_____

_____

4. What is another major effect of hurricanes?

_____

_____

5. What might you do to prepare for a hurricane?

_____

_____

Vocabulary

Directions Write the vocabulary word that best matches each definition below.
One word is used twice.

Check the Words You Know
___anemometer   ___atmosphere   ___barometer ___Doppler radar   ___hygrometer   ___meteorologists ___radiosondes   ___troposphere   ___weather forecasts

1. devices carried into the atmosphere by a balloon
   that use radio to gather and send data   _____

2. method of tracking the movement of weather systems   _____

3. device for measuring air pressure   _____

4. device for measuring the speed of wind   _____

5. device for measuring humidity   _____

6. predictions about weather in the near future   _____

7. the layer of atmosphere where weather occurs   _____

8. scientists who study and predict the weather   _____

9. the lowest, most dense layer of atmosphere   _____

10. air that surrounds Earth   _____

Directions Select two vocabulary words and use each in a sentence below.

11. _____

    _____

12. _____

    _____

The Medicine Harvest

SUMMARY This story is about a Native American boy and his grandfather from the Chumash tribe. They take a journey to gather healing plants because they are worried that the new Spanish people settling in the area will bring sickness to the Native American tribes.

LESSON VOCABULARY

cultivated   idly
ominous   purify
quell   urgency

INTRODUCE THE BOOK

INTRODUCE THE TITLE AND AUTHOR Discuss with students the title and the author of *The Medicine Harvest*. Based on the cover illustration, ask students to imagine what the book will be about.

BUILD BACKGROUND Discuss what students know about different plants and their uses. Ask them if they know plants that may harm them, such as poison ivy. You may want to prompt them with examples of plants that have healing effects, such as aloe, which is used to soothe burns.

PREVIEW/USE PHOTOGRAPHS As students preview the book, ask them to look at the photographs and guess what they think the book will be about. Draw their attention to the photograph on page 7. Ask them what clues it gives about the book's theme.

READ THE BOOK

SET PURPOSE Have students set a purpose for reading *The Medicine Harvest*. Prompt them to think about the important healing effects of plants.

STRATEGY SUPPORT: INFERRING Have students read through page 6 and then pause. Ask them to look at the photograph on page 7 and then, based on what they read, have them *infer* why the Spanish might have moved to that land. Remind them that *inferring* is using the facts and details you read in a story to make a guess about information that the author didn't mention. Ask them to explain their inference.

COMPREHENSION QUESTIONS

PAGE 4 What is the setting? *(hills full of wildflowers, weeds, and various plants)*

PAGE 15 What words or phrases on this page help you visualize the setting? *(Beautiful, twisted oaks make patterns against the yellow grass and blue sky. The autumn sun releases the rich smell of the grass.)*

PAGE 18 What conclusion can you draw about Red Hawk's future responsibilities? *(Possible response: He will teach the others about the healing benefits of plants.)*

PAGE 20 What are the healing benefits of toloache? *(It strengthens the body, cleans the blood, and dull one's pain.)*

PAGE 24 What is the theme? *(Answers will vary but may include: Natural ways of healing have been with us for a long time and may be threatened by modern civilization.)*

REVISIT THE BOOK

READER RESPONSE

1. 1500s, a hill on the California coast; answers will vary.
2. Possible response: The village will get sick from the illnesses of the Spanish, and Red Hawk will heal the people.
3. *'ap* means *home* because the context says it is where he and the boy live; from the grandfather's urgency, you know *idly* means to stand and do nothing
4. Possible response: Many will become sick.

EXTEND UNDERSTANDING Discuss with students the two main characters in this story, Bent Oak and Red Hawk. Start a discussion about each of the character's traits. Prompt students to point to places in the book that tell about these traits.

RESPONSE OPTIONS

WRITING Suggest students imagine what it would be like to live in a time when there were no drugstores or hospitals. Ask them to write a list of ways they could stay healthy without the use of today's drugs. Prompt them to think of things like eating fruits and vegetables and exercising.

SCIENCE CONNECTION

TIME FOR Science

Students can learn more about the healing benefits of plants by researching them on the Internet or in the library. Encourage them to use a graphic organizer to write a short list of some of the plants they learn about and to describe their healing benefits.

Skill Work

TEACH/REVIEW VOCABULARY

Have students look up each word in a dictionary and write the definitions. Then have them write the base word of each word with suffixes. Ask them how adding a suffix changes each word's meaning.

ELL Have students write each vocabulary word and its definition on a sheet of paper. Then have students write the words and their definitions in their home language. Ask them if there are similarities between English words and words in their home language.

TARGET SKILL AND STRATEGY

SETTING AND THEME Remind students that *setting* is the time and place in which a story occurs. As students read, ask them to write down the setting of the story and have them ask themselves if the theme depends on the setting of the story. Remind students that *theme* is the underlying meaning of a story—a "big idea" that stands on its own outside a story. As students read, have them answer the following question: What does the author want me to learn from reading this story?

INFERRING Review that *inferring* means to make a guess from evidence and reasoning about the text rather than from direct statements by the author. Remind students that understanding the actions of a character can help *infer* something about his or her personality and future actions. For example, throughout this story, Bent Oak asks Red Hawk about different plants and their healing powers. Red Hawk works hard to remember them all. Students can use this information to infer the kind of medicine man he will be in the future. After reading the story, ask students what inference they made about Bent Oak.

ADDITIONAL SKILL INSTRUCTION

DRAW CONCLUSIONS Remind students that *drawing a conclusion* is making a decision after thinking about details or facts. As they read, have students think about the future of these Native American tribes. Ask students what conclusions they can draw about the future of the Native Americans in this book, based on what they read.

Setting and Theme

- **Setting** is the time and place in which a story occurs.
- **Theme** is the subject or idea that a story is about.

Directions Based on your understanding of *The Medicine Harvest*, answer the questions below.

1. What is the setting of the story?

_____

_____

2. What is the story's theme?

_____

_____

_____

3. Does the theme depend on the setting of the story? Why or why not?

_____

_____

_____

Vocabulary

Directions Write each vocabulary word next to its definition.

```
┌─────────────────────────────────────────────┐
│         Check the Words You Know             │
│   ___cultivated        ___idly               │
│   ___ominous           ___purify             │
│   ___quell             ___urgency            │
└─────────────────────────────────────────────┘
```

1. to clear from imperfection _____

2. the state of needing immediate attention _____

3. loosened the soil around plants _____

4. to quiet, pacify _____

5. foreboding _____

6. inactively _____

Directions Write four sentences using as many vocabulary words as you can.

7. _____

_____

8. _____

_____

9. _____

_____

10. _____

_____

The Journey of African American Athletes

SUMMARY This book traces the history of African Americans in sports in the United States. Before 1945, African Americans were not allowed to play in most professional sports. This book looks at individual athletes who were able to break through the race barrier and set an example for others who follow. Some of the athletes profiled include Satchel Paige, Willie O'Ree, Jackie Robinson, Jesse Owens, Hank Aaron, and Tiger Woods.

LESSON VOCABULARY

adversity	amateur
discrimination	inferior
integrated	prejudiced
prohibited	taunts

INTRODUCE THE BOOK

INTRODUCE THE TITLE AND AUTHOR Discuss with students the title and the author of *The Journey of African American Athletes*. Based on the title and the cover photographs, ask students what they imagine this book will be about.

BUILD BACKGROUND Have students name some famous African American athletes. Ask them if they knew there were times when African Americans were not allowed to play professional sports. Ask students what it would be like to be prevented from doing what they wanted to do because of the color of their skin.

PREVIEW/USE TEXT FEATURES Have students look at the section headings and the photographs and discuss how these text elements help organize the book. Ask students how the section headings may help them understand what this book may be about.

READ THE BOOK

SET PURPOSE Have students set a purpose for reading *The Journey of African American Athletes*. Students' interest in sports can help guide this purpose. As students read, suggest they take notes that might provide answers to any questions they could have about the subject.

STRATEGY SUPPORT: ASK QUESTIONS Revisit how asking questions before and during reading can help keep the reader engaged with the information in the text. Then discuss how asking questions after reading can also help them check comprehension and solidify what they've learned. For example: *What did I learn about African American athletes that I didn't know before?*

COMPREHENSION QUESTIONS

PAGE 4 Satchel Paige had names for some of his pitches. Name a few. *(bee ball, trouble ball, Long Tom)*

PAGE 6 Who was the first African American to play professional basketball? *(Earl Lloyd)*

PAGE 7 Pro football was integrated from 1920 until 1933. What happened from 1934 to 1946? *(African Americans were barred from football.)*

PAGE 8 What was unique about Willie O'Ree? *(He was the first African American to play ice hockey, and he was blind in one eye.)*

PAGE 12 How did Jackie Robinson respond to threats and taunts after he started playing for the Brooklyn Dodgers? *(He didn't get angry or answer back.)*

PAGE 19 Who has made more money playing golf than anyone in history? *(Tiger Woods)*

REVISIT THE BOOK

READER RESPONSE

1. Possible responses:

Satchel Paige: Fact—pitched twenty-nine games in one month; Opinion—many baseball experts have hailed him as the best pitcher ever.

James Bell: Fact—centerfielder who tore around the basepaths with blazing speed; Opinion—perhaps the fastest base runner ever.

Josh Gibson: Fact—greatest hitter in baseball history; Opinion—would have eclipsed Babe Ruth.

Earl Lloyd: Fact—first African American man to play in the NBA; Opinion—had played college basketball brilliantly.

Joe Lillard: Fact—was great at catching, running, and kicking; Opinion—a sports reporter said Lillard was one of the best football players he had ever seen.

Jackie Robinson: Fact—played first major league game on April 15, 1947; Opinion—one of the best examples of an African American athlete who faced these challenges.

Jesse Owen: Fact—won four gold medals at the 1936 Olympics; Opinion—one of the best track and field athletes ever.

Hank Aaron: Fact—elected to the Baseball Hall of Fame in 1982; Opinion—one of the best major league baseball players of all time.

Suki Horton: Fact—never has there been an African American competitor in skiing; Opinion—many people think Suki Horton will be the first

2. Responses will vary.

3. Possible response: Professional hockey was not integrated until the late 1950s.

4. Possible response: The photograph shows that baseball had been integrated.

EXTEND UNDERSTANDING Discuss with students how sections in the book can help organize complicated material. Go over the sections with students and discuss what material is in each and why. Ask students how they can tell what each section is going to be about. Guide them to see that the next section is a progression.

RESPONSE OPTIONS

WRITING Ask students

Skill Work

TEACH/REVIEW VOCABULARY

To reinforce the contextual meaning of the word *discrimination* on page 3, discuss with students how the phrase "or unfair treatment" suggests the meaning of *discrimination*. Ask students to skim through the text, locate other vocabulary words, and identify the context clues that suggest meaning.

ELL Ask students to skim the story and write down any unfamiliar words. Suggest they look the words up in the dictionary and write the meanings in their notebooks.

TARGET SKILL AND STRATEGY

FACT AND OPINION Remind students that a statement of *fact* is a statement that can be proven true or false, and a statement of *opinion* is someone's judgment. A statement of opinion cannot be proven true or false. Have students point out statements of fact and opinion they find as they read the book *The Journey of African American Athletes*.

ASK QUESTIONS Remind students that asking their own questions before, during, and after they read will help them actively engage with the material. It will also help them reflect on what they read, identify the author's purpose, and separate statements of fact from statements of opinion. Offer as examples such questions as *How did the author organize the information? What is the author trying to say here? Could I turn this information into a story or movie?*

ADDITIONAL SKILL INSTRUCTION

CAUSE AND EFFECT Remind students that a *cause* is why something happened, while an *effect* is what happened. Explain that sometimes there are no clue words, such as *since*, *thus*, *as a result*, *therefore*, or *consequently*, to help us figure out what happened and why. Also, sometimes the cause is not directly stated, and we need to think on our own about why something happened.

Fact and Opinion

- A statement of **fact** can be proven true or false by reading, observing, or asking an expert.
- A statement of **opinion** is a judgment or belief. It cannot be proven true or false but can be supported or explained.

Directions Read the following passage. Decide which sentences are statements of fact and which sentences are statements of opinion. Then complete the chart below.

> Exclusion from sports was not the only challenge African American athletes faced. Many were called rude names and threatened in person, by phone, and by mail. But Tiger Woods has not faced as many obstacles as earlier African American athletes.
>
> From an early age, Tiger displayed great athletic skill. By the time he was two, he was hitting golf balls. Tiger has achieved some amazing records. But perhaps what is most impressive about his golf career is this: Although there have been African American golf champions in the past, Woods remains the only African American golfer who regularly competes in professional golf tournaments.

Statements of Fact	Statements of Opinion

Vocabulary

Directions Draw a line from each word to its definition.

```
┌──────────────────────────────────────────┐
│        Check the Words You Know            │
│                                            │
│   ___adversity          ___amateur         │
│   ___discrimination     ___inferior        │
│   ___integrated         ___prejudiced      │
│   ___prohibited         ___taunts          │
└──────────────────────────────────────────┘
```

1. adversity   jeers; mocking or insulting remarks

2. amateur   below most others; low in quality

3. taunts   condition of misfortune or distress

4. discrimination   forbidden by law from doing something

5. inferior   when a public place or group has been opened to all races

6. integrated   someone who plays something for pleasure, instead of for money or as a profession

7. prejudiced   having an unreasonable dislike for someone or something

8. prohibited   act of showing an unfair difference in treatment

Directions Select four vocabulary words and use each in a sentence.

9. _____
   _____

10. _____
    _____

11. _____
    _____

12. _____
    _____

The Land of Opportunity

SUMMARY Many people left their homes overseas and came to the United States in the early 1900s. They had dreams of making good money and having a better life. The road to a better life was filled with hard times and disappointment. For most, the journey was worth the effort.

LESSON VOCABULARY

barracks	citizens
detainees	emigrate
interpreter	naturalized
steerage	tenements

INTRODUCE THE BOOK

INTRODUCE THE TITLE AND AUTHOR Discuss with students the title and the author of *The Land of Opportunity*. Based on the title, ask students what kind of information they think this book will provide. Tell them that this is a nonfiction book, and ask them to name other nonfiction books they have read. Discuss elements of nonfiction.

BUILD BACKGROUND Discuss with students what challenges they think immigrants might have experienced. Have them think about a time when they tried something new or difficult. Ask: Was the experience what you expected?

PREVIEW/USE TEXT FEATURES Ask students to look at the photos in the book and read the captions. Draw their attention to the chart on page 7 to show them the massive number of people who immigrated to the U.S. As a class, summarize what students think the book will teach them.

READ THE BOOK

SET PURPOSE Have students set a purpose for reading *The Land of Opportunity*. Encourage them to think about the causes and effects of immigration as they read.

STRATEGY SUPPORT: SUMMARIZE Have students review the sentences they wrote that summarize each section. Then have them write a short summary of the book based on those sentences. Ask students to evaluate whether they wrote a good summary of the main ideas.

COMPREHENSION QUESTIONS

PAGE 4 Why did immigrants move to America? *(They wanted a better life, more money, freedom from their own governments.)*

PAGE 7 Name some countries immigrants came from initially. *(Italy, Hungary, Russia, Germany, England, Canada, Ireland, Sweden)*

PAGE 12 What was life like for immigrants? *(They had little money and lived in run-down, crowded tenements.)*

PAGE 18 Make a general statement about education for immigrant children. *(Most immigrant children had a difficult time getting an education because there were no schools in their homelands, and their parents didn't want them to get an education in the United States.)*

REVISIT THE BOOK

READER RESPONSE

1. Cause: Many Americans on the West Coast thought that the Chinese immigrants were taking jobs away from them. Effect: Many Chinese immigrants were held at Angel Island for a long time.
2. Immigrants had to wait for one year. They also had to pass a test that asked them questions about United States history and how the government worked.
3. Sample sentences: The family decided to emigrate from Russia to the United States. What year did you immigrate to our country?
4. Responses will vary.

EXTEND UNDERSTANDING Ask students to look at the photographs in this book and to explain how the pictures help them better understand the story.

RESPONSE OPTIONS

WRITING Have students imagine that they are an immigrant child. Have them write a letter to a friend or relative back home, listing things they miss about their home country and things they like about their new country.

SOCIAL STUDIES CONNECTION

Time For SOCIAL STUDIES

Encourage students to learn more about how immigrants become citizens today by finding a book or Internet article about the subject. Encourage them to find samples of the test that immigrants must take to become citizens. How many of the questions can the class answer correctly?

Skill Work

TEACH/REVIEW VOCABULARY

Divide students into small groups. Have each group choose a vocabulary word and write a sentence using that word. Each group writes its sentence on the board, leaving a blank where the vocabulary word should go. Have other groups guess which vocabulary word completes the sentence.

ELL Have students list vocabulary words and then write them in their home language.

TARGET SKILL AND STRATEGY

CAUSE AND EFFECT Remind students that *cause* tells why something happened and *effect* tells what happened. As students read, have them use a graphic organizer to list reasons why immigrants came to the United States and what happened as a result.

SUMMARIZE Remind students that when they *summarize*, they boil a story down to its most important points. As they read, have them write a sentence that summarizes each section. Remind students that summarizing can often help them organize the main causes and effects in a story.

ADDITIONAL SKILL INSTRUCTION

GENERALIZE Remind students that sometimes when you read, you are given ideas about several things or people and you can make a statement about all of them together. This statement is called a *generalization*. Valid generalizations are accurate or true. Have students look at the picture on page 6 and make a generalization about the immigrants' voyage to America.

Cause and Effect

- A **cause** tells why something happened.
- An **effect** tells what happened.

Directions Answer the following questions.

1. What caused many people to leave their homes and come to the United States?

_____

_____

2. What effect did immigration have on New York?

_____

_____

3. What caused immigrants to work so hard?

_____

_____

4. What caused immigrant neighborhoods to spring up in many major cities?

_____

_____

5. What effect did crowded, run-down tenements have on immigrants?

_____

_____

Directions Write whether the following are causes or effects of immigration.

6. Immigrants were poor in their home countries. _____

7. So many people immigrated to New York that it became overcrowded. _____

8. Children were given a better education in America. _____

9. America provided freedom from a harsh government. _____

10. Immigrants heard that America was the land of opportunity. _____

Vocabulary

Directions Write the vocabulary word that matches each defintion.

Check the Words You Know

___barracks   ___citizens   ___detainees   ___emigrate
___interpreter   ___naturalized   ___steerage   ___tenements

1. _____ part of the ship occupied by passengers traveling at the cheapest rate

2. _____ people who are members of a nation

3. _____ to leave your own country to settle in another

4. _____ buildings that are divided into sets of rooms occupied by separate families

5. _____ someone who orally translates from one language to another

6. _____ people who are kept from moving forward; delayed

7. _____ having been made a citizen of a country by an official act

8. _____ group of buildings for people to live in, usually in a fort or camp

Directions Write two sentences using at least two vocabulary words in each.

9. _____

_____

10. _____

_____

Our Essential Oceans

SUMMARY The ocean is a vast resource for food, such as fish and seaweed. It's also a resource for salt, fresh water, and electric power. Future uses for the ocean may include using small life forms to trap carbon dioxide, which causes global warming. The many resources that the ocean provides are explored in this book.

LESSON VOCABULARY

atmosphere	distill
ecosystems	hydroelectric
shellfish	solar
tumors	turbines

INTRODUCE THE BOOK

INTRODUCE THE TITLE AND AUTHOR Discuss with students the title and the author of *Our Essential Oceans.* Based on the title, ask students to say what they think the book will be about. Have them examine the photo on the cover of the book to help them understand the meaning of the title.

BUILD BACKGROUND Ask students to explain the meaning of the term *natural resources.* Have them list some natural resources. Ask: What resources do you think the sea provides?

ELL Have more proficient students work with less-proficient students to list natural resources that they know. More proficient peers can record responses or suggest language. Together have students list the resources they can think of that the oceans provide.

PREVIEW/USE TEXT FEATURES As students preview the book, invite them to notice the photos, and the diagrams on pages 11 and 17. Ask them to talk about how these kinds of text features give the reader different kinds of information.

READ THE BOOK

SET PURPOSE Have students set a purpose for reading *Our Essential Oceans.* Students' interest in ways of using the ocean as a resource should guide this purpose. Ask students, as they read, to think about traditional as well as future ways of using the ocean.

STRATEGY SUPPORT: VISUALIZE Have students create a five-column chart with these headings: sight, sound, taste, touch, smell. Have students choose one section in the book and list all the sensory details from that section under one of the headings on their chart. Ask them to talk about how sensory details help readers to *visualize* important information.

COMPREHENSION QUESTIONS

PAGE 3 What percent of Earth's surface is ocean? *(more than seventy percent)*

PAGE 6 Why are many people eating more fish today than before? *(for a healthier diet)*

PAGE 8 What can you conclude about fish pens located close to shore? *(They pollute the water near the shoreline and the coast.)*

PAGE 12 How is electricity generated using the tides? *(A dam with gates and turbines is built across a bay. Seawater rushing in turns the turbines and creates electricity.)*

PAGE 16 What are phytoplankton? *(small ocean life forms that convert sunlight and carbon dioxide into food through photosynthesis)*

REVISIT THE BOOK

READER RESPONSE

1. Possible responses: Edible bounty: oysters, clams, shrimp, catfish, salmon, seaweed; Inedible bounty: chemicals from sea squirts and sponges, Both: fishmeal/fish protein concentrate (FPC), seawater/sea salt

2. Possible response: Some people might be worried because so many fish together near the shore could pollute the waters. The fish produced in such a pen might not be healthy. Others might think it's exciting because, if done properly, fish farming could increase the world's fish supply.

3. the plants and animals that live in a specific environment; scientists worry that new technologies will harm these ocean ecosystems and upset the balance of nature.

4. Most are probably very dry countries without many sources of fresh water.

EXTEND UNDERSTANDING Invite students to look at the diagram on page 17. Ask them how this diagram helps them understand how carbon dioxide traps the sun's heat and warms the Earth. Ask them to explain how this diagram helps support the main idea of this section.

RESPONSE OPTIONS

WRITING Invite students to evaluate the conclusions they jotted down as they read the book. Have them choose one conclusion which seems valid and have them write a paragraph about it, explaining why they think it is a valid conclusion. Have them use facts from the book to support their conclusion.

SOCIAL STUDIES CONNECTION

Time For SOCIAL STUDIES

Students can learn more about ocean wind farms by going to the library or using the Internet. Have them find out where some wind farms are actually located. Ask: How much electricity do these wind farms actually provide? Challenge them to find out what ecological risks wind farms pose. Some students may wish to draw pictures of wind farms at sea.

Skill Work

TEACH/REVIEW VOCABULARY

To reinforce the contextual meaning of the word *distill,* have students read the paragraph on page 11. Ask: What words help you understand the meaning of the word *distill?* Continue in a similar fashion with the other vocabulary words.

TARGET SKILL AND STRATEGY

COMPARE AND CONTRAST Remind students that to *compare* means to look for how things are similar; to *contrast* means to look for how they are different. This book discusses how oceans are used as resources for food, energy, and transportation. Have students compare and contrast ocean resources with the same resources used on land. For example, have them explore the similarities and differences between aquaculture and agriculture.

VISUALIZE Remind students that to *visualize* is to create a picture in the mind as one reads. Authors use images and sensory details to help readers visualize people, places, and things. Explain that images are word pictures. Sensory details appeal to one of the five senses: sight, hearing, smell, touch, or taste. Invite students to jot down images or sensory details that they find to be particularly effective. Have them think about what conclusions might be drawn from these details.

ADDITIONAL SKILL INSTRUCTION

AUTHOR'S PURPOSE Remind students that the *author's purpose* is the reason or reasons an author has for writing. Authors often have more than one purpose for writing. Four common reasons are to persuade, to inform, to entertain, and to express something. Invite students to make a four-column chart listing the four purposes for writing. As they read, have them jot down notes in the appropriate columns to show the author's purpose.

Compare and Contrast

- To **compare** is to tell how two or more things are alike or different.
- To **contrast** is to tell how two or more things are different.

Directions Refer to *Our Essential Oceans* to answer the questions below.

1. How is aquaculture similar to agriculture?

_____

_____

_____

2. What types of aquaculture products are China, Japan, Russia, Europe, and North America known for?

_____

_____

_____

3. How is using the ocean as a source of electricity different from other sources of electricity?

_____

_____

_____

4. Ocean wind farms are being developed that are similar to wind farms used on land. Why do some people object to ocean wind farms?

_____

_____

_____

5. Why do some people prefer traveling on an ocean liner to traveling by airplane?

_____

_____

_____

Vocabulary

Directions Choose a word from the box to complete the chart.

> ### Check the Words You Know
>
> ___atmosphere   ___distill   ___ecosystems   ___hydroelectric
> ___shellfish   ___solar   ___tumors   ___turbines

	Root Word	**Word**	**Definition**
1	*skelti* + *piscis,* which means "to split + fished"		edible ocean animals such as clams, shrimps, and lobsters
2	*tumere,* which means "a swollen or distended part"		abnormal growths
3	*atmos* + *sphaera,* which means "vapor + sphere"		the air surrounding Earth
4	*turba,* which means "confusion"		spinning engines that create electricity
5	*oikos* + *systema,* which means "house + to combine"		groups of plants and animals and the environments they live in
6	*de* + *stillare,* which means "out of + to drip"		to purify a liquid

Directions Write a short paragraph about *Our Essential Oceans,* using the words *hydroelectric* and *solar.*

_____

_____

_____

_____

_____

The Most Dangerous Woman in America

SUMMARY Students read about Mary Harris Jones, a seamstress known as Mother Jones by the workers whose rights she fought to obtain.

LESSON VOCABULARY

deplorable	famine
humane	indefinitely
lavish	oppressive
regulated	resolute
staunch	

INTRODUCE THE BOOK

INTRODUCE THE TITLE AND AUTHOR Discuss the title and author of *The Most Dangerous Woman in America*. Based on the title and the photograph on the cover, ask students to describe what they think this book might be about. Ask students why someone might describe the woman in the photograph as dangerous.

BUILD BACKGROUND Explain that before the 20th century most workers had few rights or benefits. Many, including young children, worked long hours in dangerous conditions, without paid holidays, vacation, or other benefits. Later, union organizers tried to improve working conditions, often resorting to strikes to achieve their goals.

PREVIEW/USE TEXT FEATURES After students have previewed the book, discuss what they think the selection is about. Ask: What information can readers learn simply by looking at the photographs and illustrations, as well as by reading the captions?

READ THE BOOK

SET PURPOSE Have students set a purpose for reading *The Most Dangerous Woman in America*. Ask them to think about why she was considered dangerous.

STRATEGY SUPPORT: INFERRING Tell students that good readers use their background knowledge and experience as well as clues in a text to read between the lines, or make inferences. Have students infer why readers might be surprised by the last sentence on page 3, and how they made the inference.

COMPREHENSION QUESTIONS

PAGE 3 How did Mary Jones' appearance belie her nickname as the most dangerous woman in America? *(She was small and grandmotherly in appearance, rather than vigorous or threatening.)*

PAGE 4 Which experiences may have helped Mary Jones develop a fighting spirit at an early age? *(Possible response: watching British soldiers bully citizens in her native Ireland, being the granddaughter of a freedom fighter, marrying a union member)*

PAGES 7–8 Describe the two tragedies that changed Mary Jones' life. *(Her husband and four children died of yellow fever. Then everything she owned was destroyed in the Great Chicago Fire.)*

PAGES 8 How did the changes in Mary Jones' life lead her to become active in trying to secure better working conditions? *(Possible response: Once she lost everything she had, she probably was more sympathetic to the conditions of poor working people.)*

PAGES 10, 14, 15 How does seeing the young boy in the parade seem to affect Mary? *(Possible response: She could tell how hard the boy has worked, and seemed to be energized by the cause she had taken on.)*

REVISIT THE BOOK

READER RESPONSE

1. born in Ireland; husband and children died of yellow fever; lost all her possessions in the Great Chicago Fire; joined union cause; supported Eugene Debs in the Pullman strike; supported the silk strike; organized the children's march; arrested in 1912; continued making appearances into her eighties

2. Possible response: A large business owner who depended on cheap labor would regard her as dangerous because unionizing would lead to greater expenses. This insight helps readers keep in mind that people have differing opinions about many events in history.

3. Possible responses: *Deplorable* means *awful* or *appalling*. *Wonderful* is the opposite of *deplorable*.

4. Responses will likely describe wretched living conditions with no luxuries, a struggle to meet basic needs, and little opportunity for fun.

EXTEND UNDERSTANDING Explain that biographies are usually written in sequence, following important events in the life of the subject. Sometimes writers begin with an important, exciting moment in the subject's life and then backtrack to describe important events that led to that key moment.

RESPONSE OPTIONS

SPEAKING Have students locate speeches given by Mother Jones, select a brief excerpt, and practice delivering the speech aloud. They can then present the speech to the class in character as Mother Jones.

SOCIAL STUDIES CONNECTION

Have students use the Internet and print sources to briefly research related topics such as the life and work of Eugene Debs and Samuel Gompers, early and current child labor laws, and labor unions.

Skill Work

TEACH/REVIEW VOCABULARY

Have students write their own definitions of the vocabulary words based on context clues in the selection. Then have them compare their own definitions with those in the Glossary on page 24.

ELL Pair proficient English speakers with English language learners to complete the vocabulary activity above.

TARGET SKILL AND STRATEGY

SEQUENCE Remind students that biographies are usually structured by relating important events in the order they occurred. These events often reveal character traits to explain a person's actions later in life. Discuss how early events in the life of Mother Jones led her to act in the ways she did later on.

INFERRING Remind students that *inferring* is using information they know from their own experience along with clues that a writer embeds in text. Ask them what they know that could help them make an inference about Eugene Debs. *(Possible response: He was so committed to his cause that he was willing to risk losing his job.)*

ADDITIONAL SKILL INSTRUCTION

GRAPHIC SOURCES Tell students that *graphic sources*, including photographs, cartoons and captions, can reveal a great deal of information about past events. Have students work with partners to select a photograph or cartoon in *The Most Dangerous Woman in America*, analyze it, and share the inferences they can make about the persons or time period shown.

Sequence

- **Sequence** is the order in which things happen. Writers may present actual events out of sequence in order to create more drama.

Directions Look back at the selection as needed to answer the following questions.

1. At what point in the life of Mary Jones does the selection begin?

_____

_____

_____

2. Why does the writer continue cutting back and forth between events in sequence and events shown in italics?

_____

_____

_____

3. What other event in Mary Jones' life might the writer have chosen to show as it was happening, in order to heighten the drama of the selection?

_____

_____

_____

Vocabulary

Directions Write each vocabulary word under the correct part of speech. Two words should be listed under two different parts of speech.

Check the Words You Know

____deplorable   ____famine   ____humane

____indefinitely   ____lavish   ____oppressive

____regulated   ____resolute   ____staunch

Adjective	Noun	Adverb	Verb

Directions Write sentences using one of the vocabulary words. Use a different vocabulary word for each sentence.

1. _____

_____

2. _____

_____

3. _____

_____

4. _____

_____

Moving to Mali

SUMMARY A young woman joins the Peace Corps, leaving her rural home in Maine for a village in Africa. While helping others, she learns to see both the similarities and the differences between her old life and her new life.

LESSON VOCABULARY

ambition
moped
simplicity
volunteer

efficiency
rummaging
thriving

INTRODUCE THE BOOK

INTRODUCE THE TITLE AND AUTHOR Discuss with students the title and the author of *Moving to Mali*. Based on the title, ask students what kind of information they think this book will provide. Let them know that Mali is a country in Africa.

BUILD BACKGROUND Inform students that the Peace Corps is an organization that sends Americans to other countries to help the people there. Discuss what kind of help people in other countries might need. Ask students if they think it would be interesting to join the Peace Corps when they are older. Discuss where they might want to go and what kind of help they might want to give. Let them know that in this book a young woman joins the Peace Corps and goes to Africa.

PREVIEW/USE TEXT FEATURES Have students skim the book for chapter headings and illustrations. Ask them to use these features to try and predict what the story will be about. Do they think the piece will be fiction or nonfiction? Why? Point out the map on page 9. Lead students to understand that it shows part of Africa. Ask them to tell you anything they might know about Africa. If possible, locate this small map area on a classroom world map.

READ THE BOOK

SET PURPOSE Have students set a purpose for reading *Moving to Mali*. Remind them what was discussed while previewing the book and building background. Some students might want to find out what it is like in an African country. Other students might be more interested in learning about what happens to the main character or what it means to join the Peace Corps.

STRATEGY SUPPORT: STORY STRUCTURE As students read, remind them to pay attention to the story structure. Explain that the author of the selection has separated the sections into chapters. Ask: How do the chapter headings help you as you read?

COMPREHENSION QUESTIONS

PAGE 7 What does Georgia say that convinces her father that it is okay for her to join the Peace Corps? (*"I'm just like you, Dad . . . I want to improve things."*)

PAGE 18 How do you think Georgia will feel during her first few days in Mali? What are you basing your prediction on? (*Responses will vary but should be text-based and should draw from pertinent, personal knowledge.*)

PAGE 22 How is the weather in Mali different from the weather in Maine? (*It is much hotter in Mali.*)

PAGE 29 Why does Moussa give Georgia the piece of fabric? (*to thank her for helping him*)

REVISIT THE BOOK

READER RESPONSE

1. Information on graphic organizer should include the weather, experiences with chickens, friendship with 11-year-old boy, and motivated people.
2. Summaries will vary, but students should include events from the beginning, middle, and end of the story.
3. You can pedal or use the motor. *Pedem* means "foot." Words include *biped, pedestal, pedestrian, pedicure, pedometer, quadruped.*
4. Responses will vary.

EXTEND UNDERSTANDING Because this story is set in two very different places, we are able to see how the character reacts to her change in setting. How a character reacts to changes lets us know a lot about him or her. With a partner, discuss how Georgia reacts to her change in setting and what that tells you about her.

RESPONSE OPTIONS

WRITING Invite students to imagine that they are Georgia in Mali. Have them write a diary entry that Georgia might write.

SOCIAL STUDIES CONNECTION

Time For SOCIAL STUDIES

Ask students to brainstorm a list of ways they can help others in their own communities. Help them use the Internet or library to find organizations that welcome student volunteers.

Skill Work

TEACH/REVIEW VOCABULARY

Have students rate the words *Know, Have Seen,* or *Don't Know* on a Word Knowledge Rating Chart. Revise the chart after students have read the book.

ELL Have students create vocabulary word cards. Students place the cards facedown in a pile and take turns picking a card and making up a riddle for others to guess the word. Provide a model or pattern for the riddle such as:
This word starts with the letter _____.
This word ends with the letter _____.
This word means the same as _____.

TARGET SKILL AND STRATEGY

COMPARE AND CONTRAST Remind students that to *compare and contrast* things means to look for how they are alike and different. Point out that although much in the main character's life will change, some things will still be familiar to her. As students read the story, have them takes notes comparing Georgia's life in Mali with her life in Maine.

STORY STRUCTURE Remind students that *story structure* is the way the author organizes the story. All stories have a beginning, middle, and end. *Moving to Mali* is also organized by chapter headings. As students read, encourage them to pause after each chapter and summarize the information.

ADDITIONAL SKILL INSTRUCTION

CHARACTER AND SETTING Lead students to tell you that a *character* is a person or animal who takes part in the events of a story. The *setting* is where the story takes place. In *Moving to Mali,* setting has a strong effect on the main character. As students read, suggest they take notes on places where they see Georgia, the main character, being affected by her setting. Afterwards, have students compare notes and use them to draw conclusions about Georgia.

Compare and Contrast

- To **compare** is to tell how two or more things are alike or different.
- To **contrast** is to tell only how two or more things are different.

Directions Use *Moving to Mali* to help you answer the questions below.

1–2. Compare Georgia and her father. How is Georgia like her father? How is she different?

_____

_____

_____

3. Contrast Georgia's home in Mali with her home in Maine.

_____

_____

4–5. Contrast the Zeroulias' garden center when they first bought it with the way it is now.

_____

_____

_____

6–7. Compare Moussa and Georgia.

_____

_____

8. How are Ibrahim and Charlie alike?

_____

_____

Vocabulary

Directions Use a word from the box to complete each sentence below.

Check the Words You Know
___ambition   ___efficiency   ___moped   ___rummaging
___simplicity   ___thriving   ___volunteer

1. Georgia started _____through the photographs looking for her favorite picture of Charlie crowing.

2. Many people love the _____of life in developing countries.

3. Georgia was impressed with the _____ with which Ibrahim made the bricks.

4. A characteristic that both Moussa and Georgia's father had in common was

   _____.

5. Costa had built an old barn and greenhouse into a popular, _____ business.

6. Georgia had become a _____ worker for the Peace Corps.

7. Georgia hopped on the _____behind Moussa.

Directions Underline the word does not belong in each set.

8. volunteer, tradesperson, professional

9. waste, effectiveness, efficiency

10. rummaging, selling, searching

11. book, moped, magazine

12. simplicity, difficulty, complexity

13. ambition, laziness, drive

14. prospering, failing, thriving

The Talker

SUMMARY Students read a fictionalized account of a young Navajo who was trained to be a Code Talker during World War II.

LESSON VOCABULARY

battalions	code talkers
communications	company
decode	military
recognition	recruitment
restrictions	stronghold

INTRODUCE THE BOOK

INTRODUCE THE TITLE AND AUTHOR Discuss the title and authors of *The Talker*. Point out the poster in the illustration and have students speculate from the poster details what the book may be about.

BUILD BACKGROUND Explain that in the first half of the twentieth century, many Native Americans lived on reservations. Some children were sent away to government boarding schools where they were forced to abandon their culture and traditions, such as wearing their hair long and speaking their native language.

PREVIEW/USE TEXT FEATURES As students preview the book, have them pay particular attention to text features including maps, labels, table of contents, chapter headings, and illustrations that contain print (pages 9, 11, and 14). Discuss what they think the story is about, based on these features and the illustrations.

READ THE BOOK

SET PURPOSE Have students set a purpose for reading *The Talker*. You might encourage them to read to discover what the title means.

STRATEGY SUPPORT: MONITOR AND CLARIFY Tell students that good readers try to make sense of their reading. They pause to evaluate their understanding by thinking of questions such as *What does this mean? Does this make sense? Do I understand this?* Looking for answers to these questions will help them clarify their understanding.

COMPREHENSION QUESTIONS

PAGE 4–5 Why was Joe so homesick? *(He missed his family and his reservation, and worried about being punished for following his familiar traditions such as speaking his language and wearing his hair long.)*

PAGE 7–8 Why does Joe struggle with the idea of joining the army? *(He's not sure he is willing to risk his life for a government that has taken away his people's freedom.)*

PAGES 10–12 What kind of special training do Joe and Sam receive at Camp Pendleton? *(They are trained in using the Navajo language to send secret radio messages.)*

PAGE 16 How do Sam and Joe feel when Sam is marched back to camp by two armed soldiers? *(They are upset that their comrades could not tell them apart from the enemy; they worry about their safety within their own camp, and believe that others do not recognize or appreciate their efforts in fighting the war.)*

REVISIT THE BOOK

READER RESPONSE

1. The author wanted to inform readers about the important role Navajo Code Talkers played in World War II.; Explanations will vary.
2. Responses will vary, but should offer a story element that was confusing, as well as a strategy the student used.
3. Possible responses: A stronghold is something that holds with strength, or a place that can easily be defended. Other interesting compound words include *trustworthy*, *classroom*, and *hummingbird*.
4. Responses will vary.

EXTEND UNDERSTANDING Explain that historical fiction uses realistic characters to convey what it was like to live in a certain period in history. The author must do extensive research about the setting, historic events, language expressions, and viewpoints common to the time a work is set.

RESPONSE OPTIONS

WRITING Have students write a short news article that might have appeared when the public was first made aware of the role of the Navajo Code Talkers.

ART CONNECTION

Have students research the photograph and sculpture depicting the raising of the flag on Iwo Jima. They can create a tableau of the scene and share information about the event with classmates.

Skill Work

TEACH/REVIEW VOCABULARY

Have students review context sentences from the selection to write their own definitions of the vocabulary words. Then have them compare their meanings with those in a dictionary.

ELL Explain that the ending *-ion* means "act" or "state of being." Have students prepare a two-column chart of vocabulary words. They can list vocabulary and other words with the ending *-ion(s)* in one column and any cognates or words with similar meanings in their home language.

TARGET SKILL AND STRATEGY

AUTHOR'S PURPOSE Remind students that authors may have multiple purposes in writing: to inform, to entertain, to persuade, and to express an idea or feeling. Discuss the author's main purpose in writing the text on page 24. *(to inform readers about actual events in history)*

MONITOR AND CLARIFY Remind students that checking their understanding as they read will help them better understand and appreciate the text. Have them tell partners about parts of the book that they did not understand as they read. Partners can offer clarification of any sections that remain unclear.

ADDITIONAL SKILL INSTRUCTION

CAUSE AND EFFECT Historical events can often be understood by identifying causes and effects. Have students identify related causes and effects in *The Talker*. For example, the government was looking for Navajo-speaking soldiers, so Sam and Joe were placed in a secret training program. Explain that in a cause-and-effect chain, one effect can cause something else to happen. Ask students to follow up with other possible effects caused by the effect you described.

Author's Purpose

- An **author's purpose** is the reason an author writes. Authors may have more than one purpose for writing. Common purposes include writing to inform, to entertain, to persuade, and to express a mood or feeling.

Directions Answer these questions about the author's purpose in writing *The Talker*.

1. The author's main purpose in writing this book is to

_____

_____

2. The author tries to accomplish this purpose by

_____

_____

3. A second purpose may be to

_____

_____

4. The author tries to accomplish this purpose by

_____

_____

5. The author includes the episode of the American soldiers thinking that Sam was the enemy in order to

_____

_____

Vocabulary

Directions Using a dictionary, create clues for the crossword puzzle below. Write each clue on the appropriate line.

Check the Words You Know

___battalions   ___code talkers   ___communications   ___company

___decode   ___military   ___recognition   ___recruitment

___restrictions   ___stronghold

ACROSS

1. _____

2. _____

3. _____

4. _____

5. _____

6. _____

7. _____

DOWN

1. _____

8. _____

9. _____

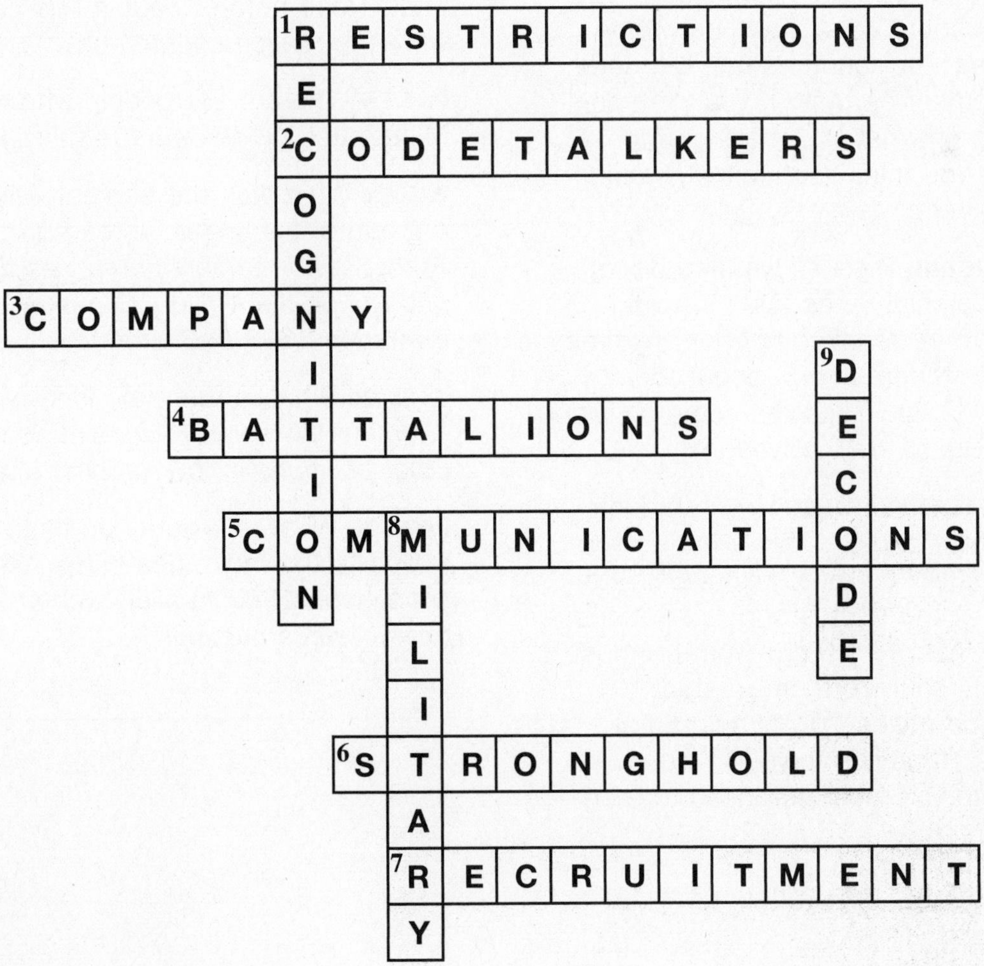

¹R	E	S	T	R	I	C	T	I	O	N	S

(Crossword grid)

1-Across: RESTRICTIONS
1-Down: RECOGNITION
2-Across: CODE TALKERS
3-Across: COMPANY
4-Across: BATTALIONS
5-Across: COMMUNICATIONS
6-Across: STRONGHOLD
7-Across: RECRUITMENT
8-Down: MILITARY
9-Down: DECODE
5-Down: CON (COMMUNICATION vertical)

The National Guard: Today's Minutemen

SUMMARY The book gives the historical background that led to the creation of the National Guard. The author also discusses the twentieth-century activities of the U.S. National Guard, including civil rights protection, riot protection, disaster relief, and international defense.

LESSON VOCABULARY

citizen-soldiers	defending
mobilize	National Guard
relief	riot
steed	troops
volunteer	

INTRODUCE THE BOOK

INTRODUCE THE TITLE AND AUTHOR Discuss with students the title and the author of *The National Guard: Today's Minutemen.* Ask them to think about what the book will be about. Discuss why countries feel the need to protect themselves. Ask: If you were going to establish a new nation, what need for protection do you think your country would have? What kind of dangers might exist?

BUILD BACKGROUND Discuss what students know about Colonial times. Ask: Why did people need to be ready to fight at any time? Discuss what students know about today's National Guard. Ask: What are some activities the National Guard are involved in?

PREVIEW/USE TEXT FEATURES Have students look at the cover photos. Ask: What do you think this book will be mostly about? Invite them to look at the photos and illustrations and captions. Ask: Which give you the most information? Encourage them to study the time line on pages 20-21. Ask: What information is unfamiliar to you? What information are you most surprised to see?

READ THE BOOK

SET PURPOSE Encourage students to set a purpose for reading that will help them remember what they have read. Suggest that as they read they take notes on the most important ideas. Remind students that writing down the dates of historical events will help them keep the sequence of events organized.

STRATEGY SUPPORT: BACKGROUND KNOWLEDGE To tap into students' background knowledge, encourage them to share what they already know about the National Guard. Encourage them to use their background knowledge as they preview and read *The National Guard: Today's Minutemen.*

COMPREHENSION QUESTIONS

PAGE 3 What question might you ask about the Minutemen before reading this page? *(Why were they called Minutemen?)*

PAGE 5 Who are the people who served as the Minutemen? *(They were farmers.)*

PAGE 6 What was the earliest evidence of a group of fighting volunteers in the United States? *(The earliest group was the Ancient and Honorable Artillery Company, which was formed in 1638 in Boston.)*

PAGE 20 What is the main idea on page 20? *(Women now serve in combat as well as in other positions in the National Guard.)*

PAGE 20 What is a detail on page 20 that supports the main idea? *(The rules were changed in 1967 to allow women to serve in roles besides nursing.)*

REVISIT THE BOOK

READER RESPONSE

1. Minutemen: mostly farmers; located in each town
   National Guard: state militias renamed to National Guard in 1916; called up to fight wars outside the U. S.
   Both: Revolutionary War; along with regular army, involved with the Civil War
2. Responses will vary.
3. *defend, defended, defending; mobilize, mobilized, mobilizing*
4. Possible response: Maine was part of Massachusetts.

EXTEND UNDERSTANDING Suggest that students review the illustration of a recruiting poster on page 9. Discuss why governments use recruiting posters. Ask: What words on this poster encourage someone to become a soldier?

RESPONSE OPTIONS

WRITING Encourage students to write a few paragraphs about why they think people decide to join the National Guard. Ask them to write about whether they would want to join the National Guard.

SOCIAL STUDIES CONNECTION

Time For SOCIAL STUDIES

Suggest to students that they may wish to go to the library to do additional research on the Minutemen. Ask: What questions do you have about the Minutemen that were not answered by this book?

Skill Work

TEACH/REVIEW VOCABULARY

Define the term *National Guard* for students. Describe how the National Guard is, and is not, like the other United States armed forces. Discuss possible synonyms for the term. Discuss possible synonyms for the rest of the vocabulary words. Explain how each synonym is either close to, or exactly like, each vocabulary word.

ELL Using clothing as props, act out the role of a person taking off his or her everyday farmer's coat or hat and donning a military type of coat or hat. Discuss the concept of being a *citizen-soldier.* Ask: Do you think you would have been interested in being a citizen-soldier during Colonial times? Why or why not? Show some pictures of National Guards doing a variety of different tasks. Ask: Was there an organization like the National Guard in your home country?

TARGET SKILL AND STRATEGY

AUTHOR'S PURPOSE Remind students that an author may write for different purposes— to inform, to persuade, to entertain, or to express feelings. Based on their previews, ask students what they think the author's purpose was for writing *The National Guard: Today's Minuteman*. Have them provide examples to support their conclusions.

BACKGROUND KNOWLEDGE Remind students that *background knowledge* is what a reader knows about a given topic, gathered from reading and from personal experience. As they preview the book, encourage students to connect their background knowledge with headings, captions, and photos.

ADDITIONAL SKILL INSTRUCTION

MAIN IDEA AND DETAILS Remind students that we look for the main idea in order to understand the most important idea that the author wishes to convey. Then we look for details to support the main idea. Discuss with students what the main idea of page 3 might be. Ask them for a detail that supports the main idea of the page.

Author's Purpose

- An **author's purpose** is the reason an author writes something. Some purposes an author may have are to persuade, to inform, to entertain, and to express a mood or feeling.
- An author may have more than one purposed for writing a particular selection.

Directions In the chart below, write the author's purpose for writing *The National Guard: Today's Minutemen* and three supporting details.

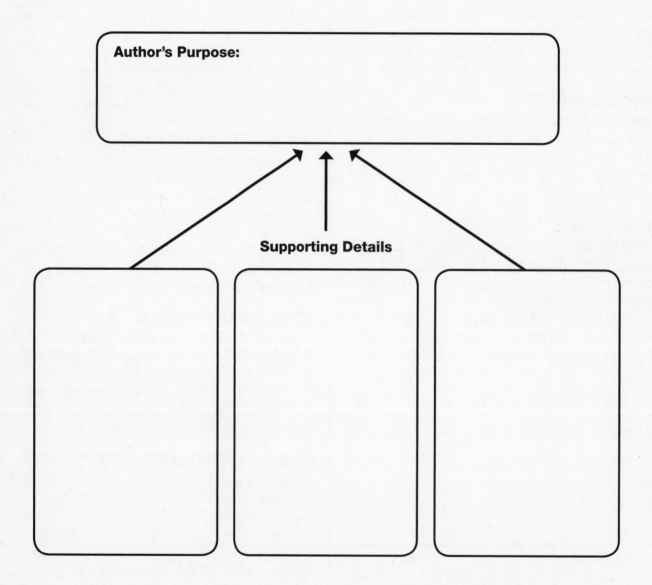

Author's Purpose:

Supporting Details

Name_____

Vocabulary

Directions Write each word in the appropriate column to show whether it is a noun or a verb. Use a dictionary if necessary.

____citizen-soldiers   ____defending   ____mobilize
____National Guard   ____relief   ____riot
____steed   ____troops   ____volunteers

Nouns	Verbs

Directions Use each vocabulary word in a sentence that shows its meaning.

1. _____

_____

2. _____

_____

3. _____

_____

4. _____

_____

5. _____

_____

6. _____

_____

7. _____

_____

8. _____

_____

9. _____

_____

Philo and His Invention

SUMMARY This book looks at an inventor named Philo Taylor Farnsworth and his invention that is used in millions of homes across the world—the television. Ironically, after legal struggles with other inventors, Philo did not get the credit when television was first introduced at the 1939 World's Fair in New York. That began to change in 1985, when a group of elementary school children in Utah petitioned the U.S. Congress to honor Philo as "The Father of Television."

LESSON VOCABULARY

envisioned	funding
furrows	manifests
mechanics	nemesis
quest	scrutiny
technology	

INTRODUCE THE BOOK

INTRODUCE THE TITLE AND AUTHOR Discuss with students the title and author of *Philo and His Invention*. Ask students to think about the title and what the book will be about.

BUILD BACKGROUND Discuss with students what they know about inventors and inventions. Ask: What do you know about how inventors protect the rights to their inventions? What problems might occur if inventors don't take the right steps to protect their inventions? Ask students to mention inventions that they use often. Discuss whether they have ever had ideas for inventions.

PREVIEW/USE TEXT FEATURES Have students preview the text by looking at the headings, diagrams, photos, and captions. Remind students that text features can help clarify what they read. Ask students how these features help them predict what the book will be about.

READ THE BOOK

SET PURPOSE Have students set a purpose for reading *Philo and His Invention*. Suggest that they consider the hard work and frustration an inventor goes through before the vision for an invention becomes a reality.

STRATEGY SUPPORT: SUMMARIZE As students read, summarizing helps them understand the important parts of the book. Have students write short summaries of each section based on their understanding of the section's main idea. Remind them that details do not belong in a summary.

COMPREHENSION QUESTIONS

PAGE 4 Who was working on an idea for the telephone before Alexander Graham Bell introduced his invention? *(An inventor named Elisha Gray was working on an idea for the telephone.)*

PAGE 5 What is a patent? *(A government-issued patent is a legal document that proves that an inventor is the rightful owner of his or her invention.)*

PAGE 10 Where did Philo get his breakthrough idea that would help to make television work? *(Philo got his idea by looking across a farm field at the rows of furrowed ground. The furrows gave him the idea of sending pictures to a receiver line by line.)*

PAGE 18 Which inventors wound up taking Philo's ideas and receiving credit as the inventors of television? *(David Sarnoff, Vladimir Zworykin, and RCA are credited with the invention of television.)*

PAGE 21 Where is the statue of Philo T. Farnsworth? What does the statue's inscription say? *(The statue is located in Statuary Hall in Washington, D.C. The inscription reads "The Father of Television.")*

REVISIT THE BOOK

READER RESPONSE

1. Possible response: He continued perfecting his television camera and receiver; He showed Zworykin how everything worked; Zworykin gave the information to Sarnoff at RCA; Zworykin's team built their own design, using Philo's ideas; Sarnoff unveils the television at the World's fair and becomes known as "Father of Television."
2. Summaries will vary, but should show an understanding of the text.
3. The farmland was cut into long, straight rows that looked like lines. This gave Philo the ideas to transmit images line by line.
4. Responses will vary.

EXTEND UNDERSTANDING Have students skim the headings in the book and discuss how the titles helped them understand the information in each section. Ask students to talk about the purpose of the section headings.

RESPONSE OPTIONS

WRITING Invite students to write a few paragraphs about a modern invention each student believes no one can live without. Suggest that they give support for their reasoning by providing examples of how the inventions are used.

SOCIAL STUDIES CONNECTION

Time For SOCIAL STUDIES

Encourage students to use the library or the Internet to research a well-known inventor, such as Thomas Edison, Henry Ford, George Eastman, or Marie Curie. Have them look for background information on the inventor, the invention, and the patent process for the invention. Invite them to share their findings with the class.

Skill Work

TEACH/REVIEW VOCABULARY

Have students play a form of Twenty Questions. Select one student to start the game by choosing a word. The remaining students should ask questions to gain clues to the word. Each question must be phrased so that it can be answered with *yes* or *no*.

TARGET SKILL AND STRATEGY

SEQUENCE OF EVENTS Remind students that we put events or ideas in sequence so that we can better understand what we have read by knowing the order in which events happen. Discuss some of the events from the book that could be put into sequence.

SUMMARIZE Remind students that to *summarize* is to boil down to its most important elements what is said in a passage. Explain that when you summarize, you tell only the most important ideas, leaving out the details. Have students use the sequence of events from above to write a short summary of the story.

ELL Have students dictate three questions about the selection to other students. Have them work together to find the answers to the questions in the book. Then have them present their questions and answers in pairs.

ADDITIONAL SKILL INSTRUCTION

GENERALIZE Remind students that when we *generalize*, we draw conclusions based on a few examples that can apply to many situations. Have students review the text on page 4 and identify a generalization made there. (*If you don't act on an idea, someone might beat you to it.*)

Summarize

- The **Sequence of Events** refers to the order of events in both fiction and nonfiction.
- Sequence can also refer to steps in a process.

Directions Write the following events in sequence.

- Vladimir Zworykin showed up at Philo's lab.

- In a flash he realized how to make television work!

- RCA had taken Philo to court over patent issues.

- A statue of Philo is added to the National Statuary Hall in Washington, D.C.

- In his lab, he successfully demonstrated the transmission of an electronic image to a receiver, or television screen.

1. _____

_____

2. _____

_____

3. _____

_____

4. _____

_____

5. _____

_____

Name_____

Vocabulary

Directions Choose the vocabulary word that best matches each definition. Write the word on the line.

Check the Words You Know

___envisioned	___funding	___furrows
___manifests	___mechanics	___nemesis
___quest	___scrutiny	___technology

1. an opponent or rival whom a person cannot beat or overcome   _____

2. close examination; careful inspection   _____

3. shows plainly; displays   _____

4. pictured in one's mind   _____

5. branch of physics dealing with the effects of forces applied to solid objects, liquid substances, or gases that are in motion or at rest   _____

6. long, narrow grooves or tracks cut in the earth by a plow   _____

7. the use of scientific knowledge to control physical objects and forces   _____

8. a search or hunt   _____

9. money set aside for a special purpose   _____

10–13. Directions. Write four sentences. Include one or more vocabulary words in each sentence.

_____

_____

_____

_____

_____

Art's Inspiration

SUMMARY Many modern artists are influenced by techniques and styles of famous artists of the past. They use these techniques, as well as their own styles, in their art. These combined styles make completely new styles of art.

LESSON VOCABULARY

baroque	cast
cubism	facade
incorporated	innovative
intricate	razing
sinuous	

INTRODUCE THE BOOK

INTRODUCE THE TITLE AND AUTHOR Discuss with students the title and the author of *Art's Inspiration*. Based on the title, ask students what kind of information they think this book will provide. Have students look at the cover illustration and tell how it relates to the book's title.

BUILD BACKGROUND Discuss with students what they know about different artists or types of art, such as paintings or sculptures. Have students share their thoughts with the class. Encourage them to name specific artists or works of art.

ELL Encourage students to describe what they know about art and artists from their cultural backgrounds.

PREVIEW/USE TEXT FEATURES As students preview the book, ask them to look at the illustrations and read the captions. Draw their attention to the various types of art and architecture shown. As a class, summarize what students think the book will teach them.

READ THE BOOK

SET PURPOSE Have students set a purpose for reading *Art's Inspiration*. Encourage them to think about the important facts in the selection as they read. Ask them to pay attention to the different types of art described, using the illustrations to enhance their understanding.

STRATEGY SUPPORT: VISUALIZE Remind students that as they read, they should combine what they already know with details from the text to create pictures in their mind. Add that they can use all of their senses, not just sight, to help them form visualizations.

COMPREHENSION QUESTIONS

PAGE 5 What is the main idea of the last paragraph under "The Story of Laocoön"? (*The emperor Titus kept the sculpture* Laocoön *on display in Rome until his death, after which it disappeared.*)

PAGE 14 What was Rodin's most famous sculpture? (*The Thinker*)

PAGE 20 Summarize the first paragraph. (*The best modern painters combine earlier art styles with their own styles to create new types of art.*)

PAGE 20 What conclusions can you draw about Pablo Picasso's cubism? (*Picasso also borrowed from artistic styles of the past to create his cubist works.*)

REVISIT THE BOOK

READER RESPONSE

1. **Main idea:** The San Carlo was revolutionary in its design. Supporting details: Instead of being flat, its facade had curves. Its design created the effect of constant motion. It influenced Frank Gehry's design for the Guggenheim Museum in Bilbao, Spain.
2. Responses will vary.
3. Possible response: *inspiration:* influence of thought and feelings on actions; *involved:* included; *incredible:* hard to believe; *individual:* single or particular; *invent:* to make something for the first time. Sentences will vary but should demonstrate students' understanding of the words.
4. Answers will vary but should include specifics as to style, subject matter, or details.

EXTEND UNDERSTANDING Ask students to look at the illustrations in the book. Ask them how the pictures help them better understand the descriptions of the art in the book.

RESPONSE OPTIONS

WRITING Have students choose one of the illustrations from the book and write a description of the artwork. Encourage them to write about the colors, textures, and the feelings the artwork evokes.

ART CONNECTION

Encourage students to look at other works of art by the artists in the book. Have them find books in the library or Internet photos. Have them share favorite works of art.

Skill Work

TEACH/REVIEW VOCABULARY

Review vocabulary words and their definitions with students. Have volunteers point to illustrations in the book that show or help explain as many vocabulary words as possible.

TARGET SKILL AND STRATEGY

MAIN IDEA AND DETAILS Remind students that the *main idea* is the most important idea about a topic. As they read, have students write a short sentence that tells the main idea of each section. Have them include a few supporting details for each main idea.

VISUALIZE Remind students that to *visualize* is to create pictures in the mind as one reads. Authors use images and sensory details to help readers visualize people, places, and things. Explain that images are word pictures. Sensory details appeal to one of the five senses: sight, hearing, smell, touch, or taste. Invite students to jot down images or sensory details that they find particularly effective.

ADDITIONAL SKILL INSTRUCTION

DRAW CONCLUSIONS Remind students that *drawing conclusions* is arriving at opinions that make sense after thinking about facts and details. As students read, encourage them to list important facts in the book and think about what conclusions they can draw from these facts. Have them write out their conclusions.

Main Idea and Details

- The **main idea** is the most important idea about a paragraph, passage, or article.
- **Supporting details** are small pieces of information that tell more about the main idea.

Directions Read the paragraph below. Then complete the graphic organizer by writing the main idea of that passage. List details that tell more about the main idea.

Michelangelo was not the first artist to borrow designs from work done in the past. Artists have always studied the art of earlier times. Often they have copied individual figures to use in their own works of art. In Michelangelo's time, this kind of copying was considered a compliment. It showed respect and admiration for older artists and contributed to the preservation of important themes from past artistic styles.

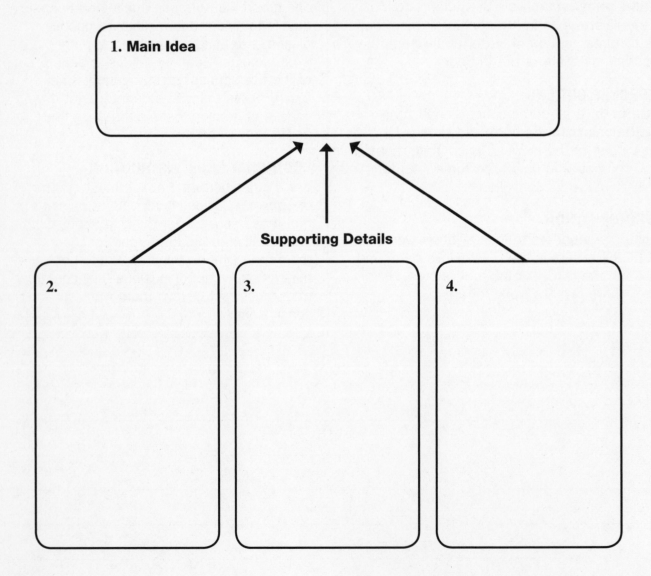

1. Main Idea

Supporting Details

2.

3.

4.

Vocabulary

Directions Write the word from the box that best completes each sentence.

> ### Check the Words You Know
>
> ___baroque   ___cast   ___cubism
> ___facade   ___incorporated   ___innovative
> ___intricate   ___razing   ___sinuous

1. Rodin _____ small figures from his doors into other sculptures.

2–3. _____ architecture uses curved, often _____ lines.

4. Rodin modeled in clay, and then he _____ the clay form in bronze.

5–6. The fine, _____ details on the building's _____ stood out in sharp contrast when the sun shone directly on them.

7. Picasso's style called _____ breaks down images into simple geometric shapes.

8–9. Creating new and _____ architecture sometimes requires

_____, or destroying, older buildings that are in the way.

Directions Imagine you were alive during the Renaissance and that Michelangelo was your friend. Write a paragraph about visiting him, using as many vocabulary words as you can.

_____

_____

_____

_____

_____

_____

_____

_____

_____

_____

What's New with Dinosaur Fossils?

SUMMARY This book explores the most current findings about dinosaurs and how opinions of dinosaurs have changed over time.

LESSON VOCABULARY

avid	carnivorous
collaborator	consensus
contention	descendants
herbivorous	olfactory bulbs
theropods	trackways
vertebrae	

INTRODUCE THE BOOK

INTRODUCE THE TITLE AND AUTHOR Discuss with students the title and the author of *What's New with Dinosaur Fossils?* Have students tell what the photo on the cover shows. What do students think they'll learn about the study of dinosaurs? Do students think this book will be fiction or nonfiction? Why?

BUILD BACKGROUND Discuss students' knowledge of dinosaurs and dinosaur fossils. Ask students if they think new discoveries about dinosaurs have occurred in recent times and how that might affect how scientists now think of dinosaurs.

PREVIEW/USE TEXT FEATURES As students preview the book, draw their attention to the map on page 15 and discuss what it shows. Then point out that the captions and the illustrations in this book contain detailed information that will help students better understand the subject.

READ THE BOOK

SET PURPOSE Have students *set purposes* for reading *What's New with Dinosaur Fossils?* Students' own interest in dinosaurs and fossils should guide this interest. To help prompt students' purposes, let them know that many significant discoveries have been made in recent years, changing the way scientists think about dinosaurs.

STRATEGY SUPPORT: PREDICT Remind students that it is important to be prepared to revise their predictions. As they read, have them write down their new predictions. Afterwards, have students compare predictions and how these changed as more information on the subject was given.

COMPREHENSION QUESTIONS

PAGE 4 Reread the first sentence. Is it a statement of fact or of opinion? *(fact)*

PAGE 12 What part of the text does this illustration help support? *(The small fossil,* Sinosauropteryx, *showed featherlike markings.)*

PAGES 16–17 How do the heading and photographs help you predict what this section will be about? Would the prediction be harder if the heading was just *Fossils?* Why? *(Answers will vary.)*

PAGE 18 What can you conclude about computer technology and paleontology? *(Possible response: Computers are able to help scientists figure out important information about dinosaurs.)*

PAGE 21 Reread the last sentence. Is it a statement of fact or opinion? *(opinion)*

REVISIT THE BOOK

READER RESPONSE

1. Possible responses: Facts—asteroids can measure up to five hundred miles in width; scientists have no direct evidence that an asteroid sent dinosaurs to extinction. Opinion: the story of these amazing animals continues to fascinate all who read and learn about them.
2. Responses will vary.
3. carnivore: animal that eats meat; herbivore: animal that eats plants
4. Possible response: the photograph of the fossil of Sinosauropteryx on page 12, which shows what might be feathers

EXTEND UNDERSTANDING *What's New with Dinosaur Fossils?* provides many photographs, illustrations, a time line, and a map to help students better understand the information. Ask students to think about how they used the graphic sources to understand the written information. Ask them to discuss what information they would not really have been able to understand or visualize without the presence of the graphic sources.

RESPONSE OPTIONS

WRITING Have students use the information in this book to write a poem about dinosaurs. Then have them create illustrations to go along with their poems.

SCIENCE CONNECTION

Invite students to read fantasy fiction or to watch a fictional film about dinosaurs. Then have them choose one of the dinosaurs from the book or movie to research. Afterwards, have students compare what their research showed with how the book or movie portrayed the dinosaur.

Skill Work

TEACH/REVIEW VOCABULARY

Have students locate the vocabulary words in the book and discuss which of them can be satisfactorily defined from context clues. (*Avid, consensus,* and *contention* have the weakest clues.)

ELL Pair proficient English speakers with English language learners to complete the vocabulary activity above.

TARGET SKILL AND STRATEGY

FACT AND OPINION Remind students that a *statement of fact* can be proved true or false. A *statement of opinion* is someone's judgment, belief, or way of thinking. Words like *believe, theory, indicate, may have been,* and *speculate* are clues that the information is an opinion and not yet proven (Although it may be a *fact* that a scientist speculated.) Other clues are subjective adjectives such as *fantastic, great, wonderful, etc.* Have students look for these clues as they read.

PREDICT Remind students that to *predict* means to tell what you think might happen next in a selection. Have students notice the headings in the selection. How is punctuation a clue to fact and opinion? (*Some headings end in a question mark, an indication that the section contains opinion.*)

ADDITIONAL SKILL INSTRUCTION

DRAW CONCLUSIONS Remind students that *drawing a conclusion* means making sensible decisions or forming reasonable opinions after thinking about the facts and details. Tell students they should be aware of conclusions that the scientists in the book make. Have students reread pages 6–7. Ask: What information did Owen use to conclude that extinct reptiles differ from modern reptiles? (*in the way their legs grew from their body*) Ask: What kind of conclusions can you make about early paleontologists? What information are you using to draw those conclusions?

Fact and Opinion

- A **statement of fact** is one that can be proved true or false.
- A **statement of opinion** is a statement of someone's judgment, belief, or way of thinking.

Directions In front of each sentence below, write whether it is a statement of fact or a statement of opinion.

1. _____ Tyrannosaurus rex was a fearsome killer that probably sprinted for short distances to catch its prey.

2. _____ Scavengers are animals that eat dead animals.

3. _____ Through their analysis of fossils, paleontologists have identified slightly over three hundred species of dinosaurs.

4. _____ One of the most fascinating (and controversial) theories regarding *Seismosaurus* is that it swung its tail fast enough to break the sound barrier.

5. _____ Cold-blooded animals cannot control their own body temperature.

6. _____ Dinosaur fossils have been found in many places around the world, including northern climates.

7. _____ Although dinosaurs are extinct today, the story of these amazing animals continues to fascinate all who read and learn about them!

Directions Look through *What's New with Dinosaur Fossils*? Find one sentence that is a statement of fact and another that is a statement of opinion. Write them below.

8. Statement of Fact: _____

_____

9. Statement of Opinion: _____

_____

Vocabulary

Directions Use the vocabulary words to answer the questions below. Each word can only be used once.

Check the Words You Know
___avid   ___carnivorous   ___collaborator   ___consensus
___contention   ___descendants   ___herbivorous   ___olfactory bulbs
___theropods   ___trackways   ___vertebrae

1. _____ What kind of animal eats only plants?

2. _____ Which word refers to certain kinds of footprints?

3. _____ What kind of person would you choose to work with you on a scientific project?

4. _____ What is your backbone made up of?

5. _____ Which word names certain meat-eating dinosaurs with sharp claws and sharp teeth that may be the ancestors of birds?

6. _____ Which word has to do with the sense of smell?

7. _____ Which word would you use for someone who is extremely enthusiastic?

8. _____ What are grandchildren and great-grandchildren?

9. _____ Which word describes lions, tigers, and other meat-eating animals?

10–11. _____ Which two words mean opposite things?

_____

The Blues Evolution

○ **MAIN IDEA AND DETAILS**
○ **TEXT STRUCTURE**

SUMMARY This book explores the ways that blues music has influenced other musical genres.

LESSON VOCABULARY

coalesced	genre
inception	mentors
prodigy	reggae
rhythm and blues	spawned
yodeling	

INTRODUCE THE BOOK

INTRODUCE THE TITLE AND AUTHOR Discuss with students the title and the author of *The Blues Evolution*. Ask if any of them has ever heard the expression "feeling blue." Explain that to "feel blue" means to feel sad or lonely. Then explain that the blues are also a kind of music. Ask students to tell you what they think the title means and what the book might be about.

BUILD BACKGROUND Play a selection of blues music. Then discuss any knowledge students have of blues music and any of the musicians named in this book. Also discuss any knowledge of the musical styles of country music, jazz, and rock and roll.

ELL Help students learn the names in English of the various instruments discussed or shown in this book; for example, *guitar*, *electric guitar*, *piano*, *trumpet*, and *saxophone*.

PREVIEW/USE TEXT FEATURES Have students look through the book. Point out the section headings that divide the information into smaller topics. Based on the section headings, what kind of information do students think the book will offer? Remind students that as they read, they should also look at the photos and read the captions to get more information on the subject.

READ THE BOOK

SET PURPOSE Have students set a purpose for reading *The Blues Evolution*. Students' interest in both music and history should guide this purpose. Students might want to learn how the history of blues music influenced some of their own favorite kinds of music.

STRATEGY SUPPORT: TEXT STRUCTURE As students read, recognizing a text's structure or organization of ideas will help them keep track of important ideas in a text. As students come to a heading, ask them what clues the heading gives about the information in that section.

COMPREHENSION QUESTIONS

PAGE 3 What is the main idea of the first paragraph on this page? (*The phrase "the blues" has been around for a very long time.*)

PAGE 4 What are some reasons workers sang in the fields? (*to ease pain and boredom*)

PAGE 7 What is distinctive about the verse structure in a Delta blues song? (*It begins with two identical lines, followed by a third, rhyming line.*)

PAGE 15 How was the group called The Carter Family influenced by blues music? (*Possible response: Their songs followed the same repeating structure as Delta blues songs.*)

PAGE 21 When was the first blues music recorded? (*1913*)

64 The Blues Evolution

REVIST THE BOOK

READER RESPONSE

1. Main idea: Blues influenced musicians of many genres. Possible responses: Details: Robert Johnson was a major influence on rock-and-roll musicians. Rhythm and blues is characterized by the same blue notes and emotional quality. English blues rock used the same structure and blue notes. Reggae was influenced by the blues sound carried to Jamaica.
2. Responses will vary, but students should include two facts about each heading in their graphic organizers.
3. Responses will vary.
4. Responses will vary.

EXTEND UNDERSTANDING Ask students how the different photographs and graphic organizers added to their understanding of the information. Which photographs did students like the best? Why? Ask them to use vivid language to describe their favorite photographs.

RESPONSE OPTIONS

WRITING Play Delta blues songs for students and then encourage students to write a few verses of blues in the Delta blues style.

SOCIAL STUDIES CONNECTION

Time For SOCIAL STUDIES

Invite students to find out more about the roots of the blues. Have them do research to find out more about how African music and culture influenced the blues. Then, have students create art to illustrate their written information.

Skill Work

TEACH/REVIEW VOCABULARY

Have partners create word cards with the vocabulary words on one side and definitions on the other. Then partners should take turns choosing cards and giving the definitions. The game should continue until both partners have correctly defined all words.

TARGET SKILL AND STRATEGY

MAIN IDEA AND DETAILS Remind students that the *main idea* is the most important idea about a topic. *Supporting details* are small pieces of information that tell more about the main idea. Let students know that the main idea of *The Blues Evolution* is that blues music influenced many kinds of other music. As students read, tell them to look for the details that support this main idea. Point out that often the main ideas in various sections of a book are the supporting details for the overall main idea.

TEXT STRUCTURE Review with students that *text structure* is the organization of a piece of writing. The author of *The Blues Evolution* organized the writing into sections with headings. Point out to students that the heading on page 4 is in the form of a question. Ask: What information might the author include in this section? *(What the blues is)*

ADDITIONAL SKILL INSTRUCTION

CAUSE AND EFFECT Ask students to define cause and effect. *(why something happened and what happened)* Read the first paragraph of page 4 aloud. Ask students to find any sentences that show cause and effect. *(Recording was difficult during the infancy of blues.)* Remind students that much of history is about cause and effect. Tell students that paying attention to cause and effect will help them better understand the history and influences of blues music.

Main Idea and Details

- The **main idea** is the most important idea about a paragraph, passage, or article.
- **Supporting details** are small pieces of information that tell more about the main idea.

Directions Read the following passage. Complete the diagram by writing the main idea of the passage. Then list supporting details that tell more about the main idea.

> Blues music has influenced other types of music. Pop music owes much of its emotional singing to blues greats such as B. B. King. Jazz music, which developed at almost the same time and nearly the same places as the blues, has borrowed heavily from the blues over the years.

Main Idea

Supporting Details

Name _____

Vocabulary

Directions Choose the word from the box that best matches each clue. Write the word on the line.

Check the Words You Know

____coalesced   ____genre   ____inception
____mentors   ____prodigy   ____reggae
____rhythm and blues   ____spawned   ____yodeling

1. _____ This music comes from the Caribbean.

2. _____ This could be the start of something.

3. _____ "So smart, and so talented—and so young!"

4. _____ A verb that means "gave birth to."

5. _____ When you sing this way, you change from an ordinary voice to a high voice and then back again.

6. _____ This popular music began in the United States and was influenced by the blues.

7. _____ This word could describe how several things came together.

8. _____ They teach—or at least provide models for you to learn from.

9. _____ A noun that means a type of artistic, musical, or literary work.

Directions Choose three words from the box and write a sentence for each of them.

10. _____

_____

11. _____

_____

12. _____

_____

Special Effects in Hollywood

SUMMARY From the early days of movies in the late 19th century, special effects—trick photography, makeup, sound effects, animation, and split screen illusions—have captivated film buffs. Many movies today rely on the computerized effects from wizards like George Lucas of *Star Wars* fame.

LESSON VOCABULARY

blue screen	cinema
continuous motion	matte painting
optical illusion	sensors
technology	

INTRODUCE THE BOOK

INTRODUCE THE TITLE AND AUTHOR Discuss with students the title and the author of *Special Effects in Hollywood*. Ask students what kind of special effect they believe is shown in the cover photo. Ask how they can tell.

BUILD BACKGROUND Ask students to discuss films they've seen that have used computerized special effects. Ask students to describe the special effects they've seen and what they liked about them. Reference the *Star Wars* films, which students will learn about in the text. They may also discuss Pixar Studios' films, such as *Toy Story* or *Finding Nemo*.

ELL Share some examples of animation on the computer or from library books. Ask students to share the names and describe the personalities of animated characters with which they're familiar.

PREVIEW/USE TEXT FEATURES Have students preview the text by looking at the table of contents, photos, captions, and subheads. Remind students that text features can help organize their reading. Ask students what they think the book will be about.

READ THE BOOK

SET PURPOSE Have students set a purpose for reading *Special Effects in Hollywood*. Some students may be interested in the early history of movies and special effects. Others may be curious how various types of modern special effects are created. Some may wish to learn about the special effects of George Lucas.

STRATEGY SUPPORT: IMPORTANT IDEAS Tell students that good readers look for important ideas as they read. Have students look through the table of contents. Explain that important ideas are oftentimes presented as chapter titles. Have students explain what these chapter titles have to do with the topic of the book.

COMPREHENSION QUESTIONS

PAGES 6–7 What was special about the first cinema? (*Large audiences could watch movies together; one of the films showed an oncoming train coming straight at the audience*)

PAGE 9 What was the impact of talkies? (*Actors could act in a more natural manner, since moviegoers could hear them talking and singing.*)

PAGE 11 How does the graphic source on page 11 help depict special effects makeup? (*It shows what Frankenstein looked like.*)

PAGE 14 How has animation creation changed in sixty-five years? (*It is often completely computerized, so filmmakers do not need to make tens of thousands of individual frames by hand.*)

REVISIT THE BOOK

READER RESPONSE

1. Possible responses: diagram, scale drawing, or photo with captions to describe it
2. Responses will vary.
3. *Optic* means "of or about the eye or sight." So *optical illusion* relates to something you see.
4. Responses will vary.

EXTEND UNDERSTANDING Focus students on pages 6–11 of the book, which feature photographs of an antique kinetoscope and three old movie posters. Ask: How do these images help you to understand the text? Would you have understood the text without them?

RESPONSE OPTIONS

SPEAKING/ACTING Have students work in groups to write and act out a 2–3-minute silent movie. Remind students to use exaggerated motions to make sure classmates understand the story line. Have each group present its silent scene. Then discuss: Now that you've practiced silent acting, what are the benefits and drawbacks of talkies?

WORD WORK Have students work with partners to draw pictures and write definitions for each of the vocabulary words. (Some of them, like *blue screen*, include two words paired for a new meaning.) Ask partners to show two or three of their drawings and definitions. Invite students to think of other examples of short phrases or idioms—simple words that, when grouped together, take on new meanings. Examples might include: *pie-in-the-sky; Web site; pot of gold.*

SOCIAL STUDIES CONNECTION

Time For SOCIAL STUDIES

Have students use the Internet or library books to research *The Jazz Singer, Frankenstein, Singin' in the Rain*, or any of the other movies or special effects techniques discussed in the book. Have students prepare short reports, using at least two graphic sources each, to present to the class.

Skill Work

TEACH/REVIEW VOCABULARY

Have students share the meanings of vocabulary words they know; then define words they don't. Have students share examples of new kinds of *technology*. Ask students where they see *sensors* used in their daily lives.

TARGET SKILL AND STRATEGY

GRAPHIC SOURCES Remind students that a *graphic source* is a way of showing information visually. Note that graphics don't stand alone but work with text to help shed light on topics that might be confusing or less interesting without graphics. Discuss types of graphics, including charts, maps, diagrams, scale drawings, and schedules.

IMPORTANT IDEAS Remind students that *important ideas* are the major parts of a topic or story. Review also that *important ideas* are supported by details. Have students keep in mind the chapter titles as they read. Have them list details from the text that support these important ideas.

ADDITIONAL SKILL INSTRUCTION

SEQUENCE Remind students that *sequence* refers to the order of events or the steps in a process. This book outlines the history of special effects and also talks about the steps in the process to create certain special effects, such as split screen. Tell students that dates and times of day are useful clues to establishing sequence. Also explain that sometimes several events or steps happen simultaneously.

Graphic Sources

- **Graphic sources** include items such as advertisements, charts, diagrams, graphs, maps, menus, photographs, recipes, and timetables.
- Use graphic sources to help you understand text and to draw conclusions as you read.

Directions Look at the graphic sources throughout *Special Effects in Hollywood*. Then answer the questions below.

1. What type of graphic source is shown on page 8?

_____

2–3. What is the purpose of the graphic source on page 8? What does it show?

_____

_____

4. How does the graphic source on page 8 compare with the one on page 11?

_____

_____

5. Why might the author have included the photograph on pages 12–13?

_____

_____

6–7. What does the photograph on page 15 show? How does it help your understanding of the text?

_____

_____

8–9. What is the graphic source shown on page 19? What conclusion can you draw from that graphic source?

_____

_____

10. What conclusion can you draw from studying the graphic sources used in this book?

_____

_____

Vocabulary

Directions Choose the word from the box that best matches each definition.
Write the word on the line.

> ## Check the Words You Know
>
> ___blue screen   ___cinema   ___continuous motion   ___matte painting
> ___optical illusion   ___sensors   ___technology

1. _____ an illusion created by showing different pictures one after another at high speed

2. _____ something that looks different from what it really is

3. _____ another term for a movie theater

4. _____ devices that react to heat, light, pressure, or other stimulations and send signals to a computer or other electronic device

5. _____ special background against which actors are filmed to create special effects

6. _____ a two-dimensional painting that serves as background for a three-dimensional stage or studio set

7. _____ the equipment, objects, or methods used to carry out a process

Directions Choose three vocabulary words. Use each word in a sentence.

8. _____

_____

9. _____

_____

10. _____

_____

Cheaper, Faster, and Better

SUMMARY Technological advances in the past twenty years, such as the creation of the personal computer, the Internet, cell phones, and DVD players, have had a huge impact on the way we run our daily lives. The Computer Age has affected everything from the way we shop and write to the way we learn.

LESSON VOCABULARY

CD-ROM	Computer Age
computer viruses	e-mail
Industrial Revolution	Internet
search engine	telecommuting
word processors	World Wide Web

INTRODUCE THE BOOK

INTRODUCE THE TITLE AND AUTHOR Discuss with students the title and the author of *Cheaper, Faster, and Better: Recent Technological Innovations.* Ask students to name some technological innovations that have made things cheaper, better, or faster.

BUILD BACKGROUND Ask students to discuss the computerized devices they use every day. Have students share stories about using the World Wide Web to complete daily activities, such as looking up weather reports or checking movie times.

PREVIEW/USE TEXT FEATURES Have students preview the text by looking at the photos and captions, the heading/subheadings, and the time line. Ask students what they expect to learn from the book.

READ THE BOOK

SET PURPOSE Have students set a purpose for reading *Cheaper, Faster, and Better.* Guide students to an interest in what life was like before computers and encourage an interest in the many inventions discussed in the text, including the Internet and World Wide Web.

ELL Ask students to discuss what the word *revolution* means to them. Share examples of inventions created during the Industrial Revolution. Ask: How might an industrial revolution differ from a political revolution?

STRATEGY SUPPORT: QUESTIONING Invite students to look at the Reader Response questions before they read. Then have them generate their own questions. As they read, have them write the answers to their questions.

COMPREHENSION QUESTIONS

PAGES 4-5 What problems did Sally confront? *(Research was tedious, overseas mail took a long time, photos had to be processed at a lab, typewriters made it hard to correct errors, etc.)*

PAGE 8 What are the benefits of word processors? *(Changing and formatting text is easy; spell-checkers are helpful.)*

PAGE 11 How are the Industrial Revolution and Computer Age similar? *(Both led to dramatic changes and inventions to simplify tasks.)*

PAGE 16 Why are search engines important for students? *(Research is simpler and less time-consuming. Instant access to global information.)*

PAGES 20–21 What conclusions can you draw about the benefits and drawbacks of computer technology? *(Benefits: speedy access to information; tasks are easier to accomplish. Drawbacks: computer viruses must be controlled; important hands-on interaction is lost.)*

REVISIT THE BOOK

READER RESPONSE

1. Advantages: can work from home, don't have to dress up for work, can set own schedule. Disadvantages: don't get to interact with colleagues, dependent on computer to get work done, could be lonely or distracting. Telecommuting is likely to be more popular.

2. Sample questions: "How did you come up with the idea for the WWW? When? Why? What is the future of the WWW?"

3. Sample: We lost our Internet connection when the power went out. Then, we couldn't surf the World Wide Web to find movie show times.

4. Answers will vary. The computers shown are different in size and appearance than the computers of today.

EXTEND UNDERSTANDING Direct students to the time line on pages 18 and 19. Note that several years – 1991, 1996, 1997, 1999, 2001, 2002, 2003 and 2005 – are not included. Have students research technological developments in these years to supplement the time line. Create a class time line with graphics (one year per page) and paste the time line around the room or assemble it into a booklet.

RESPONSE OPTIONS

WRITING Have students write a short description of a problem for which they'd like to find a high-tech solution. Then, have them describe the solution. Encourage students to draw a picture of their solution.

SOCIAL STUDIES CONNECTION

Time For SOCIAL STUDIES

Have students use the Internet or library books to research the history of the Internet or the Industrial Revolution. Have students present their findings to the class.

Skill Work

TEACH/REVIEW VOCABULARY

Have students share the meaning of glossary terms they know, then define words they don't. Make sure students understand the difference between the Internet and the World Wide Web. Ask if any students have parents who telecommute; have them describe this way of working.

TARGET SKILL AND STRATEGY

DRAW CONCLUSIONS Remind students that a conclusion is a sensible decision reached after thinking about details or facts in what you read. Drawing conclusions is the process of making those decisions. Encourage students to draw conclusions after considering the facts given in a paragraph or section of text. Encourage students to ask themselves if their conclusions make sense and to back up conclusions with information from the text or other reasons. Conclusions should be logical.

QUESTIONING Remind students that both *asking questions* and *answering questions* can help them better understand the text. Encourage students to use text features such as headings, pictures, and captions to help them pose questions. Point out that as they read, they can use information in the text and prior knowledge to answer their questions.

ADDITIONAL SKILL INSTRUCTION

CAUSE AND EFFECT Remind students that a cause is why something happened, while an effect is what happened. Explain that sometimes there are no clue words, such as *since, thus, as a result, therefore,* or *consequently,* to help you figure out what happened and why. Also, sometimes the cause is not directly stated, and you need to think about why something happened on your own.

Draw Conclusions

- A **conclusion** is a sensible decision you reach after you think about the details or the facts in what you read.
- **Drawing conclusions** means to make sensible decisions or form reasonable opinions after thinking about the details or facts in what you read.

Directions Read the paragraph below, then answer the questions that follow.

Completing tasks we now do quickly was not nearly as easy in the 1970s, when Sally was growing up. If Sally wished to do research for a report, she had to ask her parents to drive her to the library. There, she used a large encyclopedia; her parents could not afford to buy her such a set. If Sally needed to type her report, she had to use a manual typewriter. Whenever she made mistakes, she had to use a special white solution to paint over the wrong letters. Then she could retype the correct letters. When Sally didn't remember the spelling for a word, she hauled out a huge dictionary to look it up. Sally was also a movie buff. To figure out which shows she would attend, she had to wait for the newspaper to be delivered. And if she wanted to shop, her only choices were to go to a mall and endure long lines and bustling crowds or to pore over heavy catalogues. If she wanted to shop at midnight, she was out of luck!

1. What conclusion can you draw about what it was like to do homework in the 1970s?

_____

2. Give two facts or details to support your conclusion.

_____

_____

3. What conclusions can you draw about what shopping was like in the 1970s?

_____

4. Give two facts or details to support your conclusion.

_____

_____

5. Write a well-supported conclusion about how technology would have made life easier for Sally.

_____

Vocabulary

Directions Choose the word from the box that best matches each definition. Write the word on the line.

> **Check the Words You Know**
>
> ___CD-ROM ___Computer Age
> ___computer viruses ___e-mail
> ___Industrial Revolution ___Internet
> ___search engine ___World Wide Web
> ___word processors

_____ 1. when people work from home using their personal computers

_____ 2. programs, designed by people, that do damage to computers or data

_____ 3. system that allows people to review, retrieve, and modify the Web sites found on the Internet

_____ 4. a compact disc that plays on a computer's CD-ROM drive

_____ 5. a term describing the changes in technology of the 1800s that changed how people lived

_____ 6. a program that helps people find data on the Internet

_____ 7. system of sending messages using computers linked by telephone wires

_____ 8. worldwide computer network, linked by telephone lines, that is used to send messages, data, and other services

_____ 9. a term used to describe how computers have transformed modern life

_____10. computer programs that edit, store, and retrieve documents and texts

Operation Inspiration

SUMMARY In this narrative nonfiction selection, four young people are recognized for their outstanding efforts in identifying a global or local issue and then enacting a plan to make a difference.

LESSON VOCABULARY

ally	daunting	discouraged
documentary	legislation	liabilities
resources	sponsors	vulnerable

INTRODUCE THE BOOK

INTRODUCE THE TITLE AND AUTHOR Discuss the title and author of *Operation Inspiration*. Discuss the cover photographs. Ask students to tell what they think the book will be about, based on the title and cover photographs.

BUILD BACKGROUND Have students share what they already know about global and local problems. Ask them if they donate to or volunteer with an organization that helps others. Have students share their experiences. Explain that this book is about four separate students who are inspired by global or local problems and do outstanding work to make a difference.

PREVIEW/USE TEXT FEATURES Have students preview the book by looking at the photographs and reading the captions. Remind students that captions tell what the photograph is about. Have students turn to pages 22–23. Explain that these pages have ideas and activities written directly to the reader by the author. Have students turn to page 24. Remind students that a glossary works like a dictionary and provides definitions for words they may not know. Point out that each vocabulary word is highlighted within the text.

READ THE BOOK

SET PURPOSE Have students set a purpose for reading *Operation Inspiration*. Ask them to think about a global or local problem they already are aware of or one they are reading about. As students read, have them write ideas of what they can do to help make a difference.

STRATEGY SUPPORT: PREDICT AND SET PURPOSE Have students reread part of Daniel's story on page 20. Based on the statistics provided, have students predict the impact of Daniel's computer outreach program if 10, 25, or all 50 states participated.

COMPREHENSION QUESTIONS

PAGES 4–5 What were Jack's inspirations to make a difference? *(wasted restaurant food, homeless people who needed food)*

PAGES 9–12 What generalization can you make about Katherine's and her mom's efforts to provide bed nets? *(Responses may vary but make sure students understand the concept of generalization.)*

PAGE 16 How do you think Chanelle's story in a major magazine could help make a difference? *(Possible response: The magazine would reach many more people and inspire them to clean up their local area.)*

PAGES 19–20 Make a generalization about Daniel's impact on the senior citizen community. *(Responses may vary but make sure students understand the concept of generalization.)*

PAGES 22–23 What is the author's purpose for including these two pages? *(to persuade)*

REVISIT THE BOOK

READER RESPONSE

1. Responses may vary but make sure students explain why they chose those qualities.
2. Responses may vary but make sure students include ideas beyond what is in the story.
3. Responses may vary but make sure students show understanding of each word's meaning.
4. Responses may vary but make sure students show understanding of "global problem."

EXTEND UNDERSTANDING Explain to students that it usually takes a lot of hard work, time, people, and often money to address large issues and make an impact. These types of problems are not easily solved but every effort to make a difference is extremely important and sometimes saves lives.

RESPONSE OPTIONS

WRITING Have students research a global or local problem. Have them write a persuasive paper to encourage others to help make a difference. Students can use books, the internet, or interview someone connected with an organization to gather information.

SOCIAL STUDIES CONNECTION

Time For SOCIAL STUDIES

Using page 23 as a guide for a class project, have students select a local organization they would want to support if they could and follow the guidelines.

Skill Work

TEACH/REVIEW VOCABULARY

Have pairs of students create vocabulary cards. Instruct one partner to hold up a card while the other partner gives the definition. Have partners take turns holding cards and giving definitions. Students should play until partners have correctly defined all words. Students can use the Glossary to check their definitions.

ELL Have students locate vocabulary words within the text and use context clues to define each word. Students can use the Glossary to check their definitions.

TARGET SKILL AND STRATEGY

GENERALIZE Remind students that sometimes when they read, they are given ideas about several things or people and they can make a statement about all of them together. This statement is called a *generalization*. Valid generalizations are accurate or true based on the information in the story, and faulty generalizations are not. Ask students to make a generalization about each individual student featured in this book. Ask them to make a generalization about people who do outstanding work.

PREDICT AND SET PURPOSE Remind students that a prediction is what you think might happen in a story based on what you have already read or know. Have students turn to Katherine's story on pages 9–12. Point out that between April 2006 and April 2007, Katherine and her mom had raised more than $85,000. If they continued to raise that much money each year, how many nets could they have purchased and distributed by today? Predict how many more nets five years from now.

ADDITIONAL SKILL INSTRUCTION

AUTHOR'S PURPOSE Remind students that authors often write to inform, persuade, express, or entertain. Ask: What do you think Becky Cheston's purpose was for writing this book? *(to inform)* Discuss the importance of informing others about problems in the world. Discuss the impact authors can have on their audience.

Generalize

- A **generalization** is a broad statement or rule that applies to many examples. A generalization is made after thinking about a number of examples or facts and what they have in common.
- A **valid generalization** is supported by specific facts.
- A **faulty generalization** is not supported by specific facts.

Directions Based on *Operation Inspiration*, write next to each generalization whether it is valid or faulty. On the line below each generalization, write one fact from the text that supports your answer.

1. Jack had help from people in the judicial system. _____

_____

_____

2. Malaria does not affect children. _____

_____

_____

3. Everyone wanted to help Chanelle clean up Hartford. _____

_____

_____

4. Many senior citizens are eager to learn how to use computers. _____

_____

_____

5. Only large groups of people can start an organization and make a difference. _____

_____

_____

Vocabulary

Directions Choose the word from the box that best matches each definition. Write the word on the line.

┌───┐
│ **Check the Words You Know** │
│   │
│ ___ally   ___daunting   ___discouraged │
│ ___documentary   ___legislation   ___liabilities │
│ ___resources   ___sponsors   ___vulnerable │
└───┘

1. supporter of a common cause   _____

2. open to harm   _____

3. removed hope   _____

4. supporters   _____

5. abilities or supplies that can be used   _____

6. legal responsibilities   _____

7. a film based on or recreating an actual event _____

8. laws   _____

9. overwhelming   _____

Directions Choose three vocabulary words. Use each word in a sentence.

10. _____

_____

11. _____

_____

12. _____

_____

Can Humans Make a Home in Outer Space?

SUMMARY This book presents information about research on deep-space travel and the adaptations humans would have to make to sustain long voyages. It explores benefits and drawbacks of space travel and colonization. Information is included about early space voyages and scientific research on other planets.

LESSON VOCABULARY

asteroids	astronomically
contend	cycle
deflect	extraterrestrial
vegetation	

INTRODUCE THE BOOK

INTRODUCE THE TITLE AND AUTHOR Discuss with the students the title and the author of *Can Humans Make a Home in Outer Space?* Based on the title, ask students what information they think this book will provide. Do they think this book will provide both sides of this issue? Why or why not?

BUILD BACKGROUND Ask students to share what interests them about space and space travel. Ask what they think it would be like to live in outer space. Do they think it's a good idea to explore space? Why or why not?

ELL Build background for English language learners by using a map of the solar system and talking about space and space travel.

PREVIEW/USE TEXT FEATURES Have students look at the photos, captions, and headings. How do these text features help them know how this book is organized? What other text features can students find in this book?

READ THE BOOK

SET PURPOSE Have students set a purpose for reading *Can Humans Make a Home in Outer Space?* Their interest in space and space travel may drive this purpose. They may also be interested in what the future holds for the human race. Encourage students to think about their purpose throughout their reading.

STRATEGY SUPPORT: IMPORTANT IDEAS Remind students that distinguishing between *important ideas* and less-important ideas will help them remember essential information in the text. As students read, encourage them to locate important ideas in the text and find details that support them.

COMPREHENSION QUESTIONS

PAGE 8 Why do scientists think Mars is the most likely planet to support life? *(A meteorite that fell to Earth from Mars 13,000 years ago appeared to have bacteria in it. Mars has, or once had, water.)*

PAGES 10–11 Why is zero gravity a problem for humans? *(People lose muscle and bone strength; heart becomes inefficient.)*

PAGE 14 What are some of the benefits of building space colonies? *(Possible response: Escape disaster on Earth. Helpful to have experiments done in zero gravity. Learn how to harvest solar power.)*

PAGE 15 What is the topic of the circle graph? *(global power consumption)*

REVISIT THE BOOK

READER RESPONSE

1. oil
2. Responses will vary but should show an understanding of how quickly space exploration developed.
3. The roots of both words come from the Greek word meaning "star." Responses will vary.
4. Responses will vary.

EXTEND UNDERSTANDING Have students look at the picture on page 13. Discuss some of the details they can see in the picture. Based on this picture talk about what life might be like on a space colony.

RESPONSE OPTIONS

WRITING Ask students what their opinions are about space travel. Have students write a persuasive paper about whether we should or shouldn't pursue space travel. Be sure students include facts they learned from the book to support their main idea.

WORD WORK *Asteroid* and *celestial* are "space" words. Encourage students to find other space words in the text or on their own. Have them draw a picture of the solar system and include the words and their definitions.

SCIENCE CONNECTION

Have students explore space by looking at the NASA web site (kids.msfc.nasa.gov/).

Skill Work

TEACH/REVIEW VOCABULARY

Have students locate the vocabulary words in the text. Have them define each word using context clues, the glossary, and a dictionary. Then invite students to list for each word as many words as possible that have similar meanings or are related in some way.

TARGET SKILL AND STRATEGY

GRAPHIC SOURCES Remind students that *graphic sources* are graphs, maps, photographs, and diagrams that help strengthen their understanding of the text. Have students read page 18 and then look at the chart. Ask: What information is in the chart? How does the chart add to what you read in the text?

IMPORTANT IDEAS As students read, remind them to keep track of important ideas in the text. Explain that *important ideas* tell more about the topic of the passage. Have students create a list of important ideas the find in the text and add two or three details that support them. Then have each student compare their list with a partner's and explain why they think the ideas are important.

ADDITIONAL SKILL INSTRUCTION

FACT AND OPINION Explain that a statement of *fact* can be proven true or false by reading, observing, or asking an expert. A statement of *opinion* is a judgment or belief that cannot be proven true or false but can be supported or explained. Draw a T-chart on the board and label one column *Statements of Fact* and the other *Statements of Opinion*. Then ask students to discuss what they know about outer space and point out which of their statements belong in which column.

Graphic Sources

Graphic sources are graphs, maps, pictures, photographs, and diagrams that help strengthen understanding of text.

Directions Using information you learned from the book, especially page 20, show the distance between Earth and the moon and Earth and Mars above the arrows. On the lines provided below the diagram, write what scientists are learning about life in space and questions they still have. Add questions that you have.

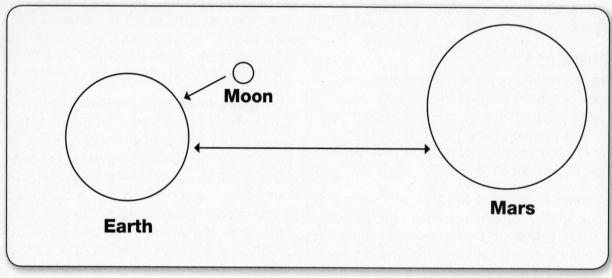

_____

_____

_____

_____

_____

_____

_____

_____

_____

Name_____

Vocabulary

Directions Fill in the blanks in the sentences below with the correct word from the box.

> ### Check the Words You Know
>
> ___asteroids   ___astronomically
> ___contend   ___cycle
> ___deflect   ___extraterrestrial
> ___vegetation

1. Scientists are studying ways to _____ debris from space before it hits Earth.

2. Astronauts must _____ with many challenges presented by space travel.

3. There are about 100,000 _____ orbiting the sun.

4. The amount of money required to build a space colony is

   _____ large.

5. The moon is on a twenty-nine day _____ as it circles around the earth.

6. Some people support space travel as a way to search for

   _____ life.

7. Human beings depend on _____ as a source of oxygen and food.

Nathaniel Comes to Town

SUMMARY Drew hates going to school, has very few friends, and hates lying about how he feels about school. Then Nathaniel, a boy he met at the beach the summer before, moves to town. Nathaniel tries to become friends with Drew, but Drew is embarrassed by him and rejects Nathaniel at first. By the end of the story, their friendship is patched and Drew feels better about school.

LESSON VOCABULARY

annoyingly	foreboding
gallantly	humiliation
jostling	skeptically

INTRODUCE THE BOOK

INTRODUCE THE TITLE AND AUTHOR Discuss with students the title and author of *Nathaniel Comes to Town*. Based on the title alone, ask students what they think the story will be about. Does the picture on the front cover give them any clues?

BUILD BACKGROUND Ask students if any of them have ever had trouble finding friends in school. What did they do to make new friends? Ask them if they have ever befriended a new student. Ask them what they look for in a friend.

ELL Have students talk about what it was like for them to be new students at a new school. What did they do to try to make friends? Was English a barrier, or were they able to communicate?

PREVIEW Encourage students to look at the chapter headings and illustrations to try to predict what will happen in this book.

READ THE BOOK

SET PURPOSE Have students set a purpose for reading *Nathaniel Comes to Town*. Students may want to pick a character to follow, such as Drew or Nathaniel. Have the students follow what happens to the character and why. They may want to take notes as they read.

STRATEGY SUPPORT: STORY STRUCTURE As students read, remind them to pay attention to the story structure. Explain that the author has separated the sections of the story into chapters Ask: How do chapter headings help you as you read?

COMPREHENSION QUESTIONS

PAGES 4–6 List all of the reasons you can find in the first chapter of the story that Drew doesn't like school. *(no friends, former friends, feeling sick)*

PAGE 8 What did Drew think of Nathaniel after spending time with him at the beach? *(He thought he was annoyingly smart.)*

PAGES 17–18 When Nathaniel has lunch with Soraya instead of Drew, what emotion does Drew feel? *(envy)*

PAGE 21 What happens when Julie tries to make dinner for their guests? *(She sets off the fire alarm.)*

PAGES 24–25 Why was Drew embarrassed by his purple basketball? *(Jeff made fun of it, which led to the end of their friendship.)*

PAGES 24–27 What happens between Drew and Nathaniel while they are playing basketball? *(They become friends again.)*

REVISIT THE BOOK

READER RESPONSE

1. It is hard to make friends and easy to feel lost. Moving to a new school can be difficult.

2. Possible responses: Characters—Drew, Nathaniel; Setting—school bus, home, basketball court; Problem—Drew hates school because he has few friends; Event 1—Nathaniel moves into the neighborhood; Event 2—Drew and Nathaniel become friends; Solution—Friendship changes Drew's outlook on school.

3. Possible responses: *skeptically*: My mother looked at me skeptically when I offered to help; *offended*: I felt offended by my sister's negative comment; *demoted*: I was demoted to junior varsity; *cavities*: I had two cavities filled.

4. Possible responses: Nathaniel makes friends by actively trying and not being easily defeated. Drew takes longer to make friends.

EXTEND UNDERSTANDING Remind students that a character is the person who does the action in the story. Review with students that you can use the details in the story to tell many things about what kind of person a character is. Ask the students to think about how Drew changes as a character. Ask: Does this relate to the theme of the story?

RESPONSE OPTIONS

WRITING Have students think back to their first day in grammar school. Have them write about how they felt. How did they try to make friends? Ask them to write about how they made friends.

SOCIAL STUDIES CONNECTION

Have students read about the Three Famous Failures on page 28. Have them choose one of the three and research that person on the Internet or at the library.

Time For SOCIAL STUDIES

Skill Work

TEACH/REVIEW VOCABULARY

Review the vocabulary words. Then play "Vocabulary Master" with students. Give them three different definitions for each vocabulary word, including one that is fantastical or silly. Have them select the correct definition and use the word in a sentence.

TARGET SKILL AND STRATEGY

GENERALIZE Tell students: "Sometimes when you read, you are given ideas about things or people, and you can make a statement about all of them together. This statement is called a *generalization*. Look for clue words, such as *most, always, all,* and *never*. Valid generalizations are accurate. Faulty generalizations are not accurate." Tell students that identifying faulty generalizations can help them tell whether an author or character is biased. Have students make their own generalization by stating how the kids at school feel about Drew at the beginning of the story. After reading, ask: Is your generalization still valid?

STORY STRUCTURE Remind students that story structure is the way the author organizes the story. All stories have a beginning, middle, and end. *Nathaniel Comes to Town* is also organized by chapters. As students read, encourage them to pause after each chapter and summarize the information.

ADDITIONAL SKILL INSTRUCTION

THEME AND PLOT Remind students that the *theme* of a story is the underlying meaning of a story and a story may have different themes. Remind them that the *plot* is the organized pattern of events. As they read, have students follow the plot through beginning, middle and end. Have them think about the climax of the story. What do they think the theme of the story is, and how does the climax relate to the theme?

Generalize

- A **generalization** is a broad statement or rule that applies to many examples. A generalization is made after thinking about a number of examples or facts and what they have in common.

Directions What are some of the difficulties faced by Nathaniel as a new student? What can you generalize about the difficulties that all new students face?

1. _____

_____

2. _____

_____

3. _____

_____

4. _____

_____

5. Generaliztion: _____

_____

Directions Based on Drew's experiences, what can you generalize about how difficult it is to help a new student find his way?

6. _____

_____

7. _____

_____

8. _____

_____

9. _____

_____

10. _____

_____

Vocabulary

Directions Fill in the blank with the word from the box that fits best.

> ### Check the Words You Know
>
> ___ annoyingly   ___ foreboding
> ___ gallantly   ___ humiliation
> ___ jostling   ___ skeptically

1. Drew viewed going to school with _____ and dread.

2. Nathaniel _____ tried to make friends at his new school.

3. The color of Drew's basketball caused him _____ .

4. In gym class, Nathaniel tried _____ for the ball.

5. Drew's sister liked to tease him _____ .

6. Drew reacted _____ to his teacher's cheerful greeting.

Directions Write a brief paragraph discussing Nathaniel's first day at school, using as many vocabulary words as possible.

_____

_____

_____

_____

_____

_____

_____

_____

_____

_____

What Makes Great Athletes?

SUMMARY This book discusses what it takes to be a great athlete. It tells about the demands of training and competing that athletes have to endure to prepare for a major competition. It also highlights various notable athletes, such as Jim Thorpe and Babe Didrikson Zaharias.

LESSON VOCABULARY

archaeologists	artifacts
Colosseum	coordination
endurance	esteem
mastery	persistence
rigorous	

INTRODUCE THE BOOK

INTRODUCE THE TITLE AND AUTHOR Discuss with students the title and the author of *What Makes Great Athletes?* Based on the cover photograph, ask students what kind of information they think this book will provide. Have students decide if this book is a fiction or a nonfiction book. Then ask them to name other books they have read in this genre.

BUILD BACKGROUND Ask students what sports they like to play or if they are on a sports team. Generate a discussion about what they think makes a good athlete. Prompt them to think of qualities like practice and determination.

PREVIEW/USE TEXT FEATURES As students preview the book, the action shots of the athletes will probably attract their attention. Ask them to read the captions that go with the photographs to give the photographs more meaning. Have them look at the photographs on pages 4–5 and ask them how they think these images will help them better understand the text.

READ THE BOOK

SET PURPOSE Have students set a purpose for reading *What Makes Great Athletes?* Students' interest in sports competitions should guide this purpose. Suggest that students think about how we can achieve many things if we work really hard.

STRATEGY SUPPORT: VISUALIZE As students read about outstanding individuals such as Babe Didrikson Zaharias, visualizing gives them a chance to imagine how a person can become great at something if he or she has determination and dedication to a goal. Ask students to imagine what it would be like to be an award-winning Olympic athlete.

COMPREHENSION QUESTIONS

PAGE 6 About how many years ago did the first Olympic games occur? *(2,800)*

PAGE 8 What conclusion can you draw about what the Ancient Greeks thought about athletes? *(They valued them.)*

PAGE 8 What details helped you come to your conclusion in the question above? *(They gave winning athletes large amounts of money, free meals, decorated jars, and even built statues of them.)*

PAGE 13 How many miles would Jim Thorpe run to get home from school? *(twenty miles)*

PAGE 15 What made Babe Didrikson Zaharias such a good athlete? *(She focused on her dream and she was strong both mentally and physically.)*

REVISIT THE BOOK

READER RESPONSE

1. Responses will vary.
2. Responses will vary.
3. spectacular; energy; hesitating; hesitate; marvel; accurate; honorable
4. Responses will vary but may include references to how athletes were treated then and now and the emphasis on running in ancient times and on team sports in modern times.

EXTEND UNDERSTANDING As students look at the photographs, ask them why they like certain ones. Ask them if the photographs help them imagine what athletes go through to compete. Draw their attention to the photographs of athletes in action, especially on pages 4 and 5. Ask students to discuss with a partner what qualities make a good athlete.

RESPONSE OPTIONS

WRITING Ask students to imagine they have to prepare for a major competition. Have them make a daily training and meal schedule to help them train for the event.

SOCIAL STUDIES CONNECTION

Time For SOCIAL STUDIES

Students can learn more about how athletes train by researching them on the Internet or at the library.

Skill Work

TEACH/REVIEW VOCABULARY

Divide students into small groups. Have each group compete to make new words from the vocabulary words by removing the suffixes or adding new ones. Have groups add up their new words and share their words with the class.

ELL Have students write each vocabulary word on a separate index card. Then have them sort the words into words with suffixes. Finally, ask them to write the root word of each word, using a dictionary if necessary.

TARGET SKILL AND STRATEGY

DRAW CONCLUSIONS Remind students that a conclusion is a sensible decision reached after thinking about details or facts in what is read. As they read, have students *draw conclusions* about what qualities a good athlete possesses, showing them by creating a graphic organizer.

VISUALIZE Remind students that to *visualize* is to create a picture in the mind. As students read, suggest that they visualize what it would be like to be a great athlete in their favorite sport.

ADDITIONAL SKILL INSTRUCTION

SEQUENCE Remind students that *sequence* refers to the order of events in both a fiction and nonfiction text. Sequence can also refer to the steps in a process. Ask students to read the following sentences from page 12 about the life of Babe Didrikson Zaharias. Then have them put the sentences in sequential order.

1. After her career as a track and field champion, she became a professional golfer.
2. By the time she was in her teens, she already knew she wanted to be the greatest athlete ever.
3. She ... easily won the javelin and the 80-meter hurdles events at the Olympics.

Draw Conclusions

A **conclusion** is a sensible decision reached after thinking about details as facts in what is read.

Directions Read the following paragraph. Then answer the questions.

Much of our interest in sports and athletes comes from our knowledge of sporting events in ancient Greece. The first Olympics were held at least 2,800 years ago, and scholars believe that such games were probably held before then. The games were held at Olympia, a center of religious ceremonies, in honor of Zeus, the most powerful of the Greek gods. Those early games were festivals that combined races with religious observances.

1. Why did the early Olympics combine races with religious observances?

_____

_____

2. Why did the Greeks think the Olympics would honor Zeus?

_____

_____

3. Where does our interest today in sporting events come from?

_____

_____

4. Do you believe that the first Olympics were held before 2,800 years ago?

_____

_____

5. Do you wish that you could have ran in the first Olympics? Why?

_____

_____

Vocabulary

Directions Write the vocabulary word that best matches each definition from the box.

Check the Words You Know

____archaeologists   ____artifacts
____Colosseum   ____coordination
____endurance   ____esteem
____mastery   ____persistence
____rigorous
---

1. large building where people watched events in ancient Rome _____

2. not giving up _____

3. great knowledge of something _____

4. items made for a special use _____

5. the strength to withstand hard work _____

6. to regard favorably or admirably _____

7. those who study ancient people and civilizations _____

8. working together _____

9. demanding _____

The Sandwich Brigade

SUMMARY Herb, Bob, and Pete are three retired men with time on their hands. When Bob comes up with an idea to help people in their area by providing them with healthy lunches, the lives of the three men change.

LESSON VOCABULARY

pondered	putter
recruit	retirement

INTRODUCE THE BOOK

INTRODUCE THE TITLE AND AUTHOR Discuss with students the title and the author of *The Sandwich Brigade*. Based on the title, ask students what they think the book will be about and what they think the title means. Ask: What is a *brigade?* Encourage students to look up the word in the dictionary. Determine the context in which the word is usually used. *(military)* Ask students if they think it will be used in this context in the book? *(No)* Why not? *(This book is not about the military.)*

BUILD BACKGROUND Discuss what students know about being retired. Ask them if they know some retired people. Ask them what these people do with their time.

PREVIEW/USE TEXT FEATURES As students preview the book, have them notice the chapter titles and illustrations. Compare these to the photo on page 28. Invite students to predict how the illustrations and the photo complement each other.

READ THE BOOK

SET PURPOSE Have students set a purpose for reading *The Sandwich Brigade*. Students' interest in senior citizens and helping people in the community should guide this purpose.

STRATEGY SUPPORT: PRIOR KNOWLEDGE Ask students if they have ever helped anybody in need. Have them share what they did and how it made them feel afterwards. Ask them what it means to be a volunteer in the community.

COMPREHENSION QUESTIONS

PAGE 4 What was Herb Battleby's former profession? *(movie reviewer)*

PAGE 8 How did Herb react when Bent threw him? *(He was angry and upset.)*

PAGE 11 How would you describe Herb's wife, Eden? *(patient, loving, helpful)*

PAGE 15 Who gave them the idea to help shut-ins? *(Herb's wife, Eden)*

PAGE 16 How do Herb, Bob, and Pete go about setting up their project? *(Bob goes after money, Pete organizes food discounts, Herb organizes volunteers.)*

PAGE 25 How did the Sandwich Brigade get to be so well known? *(An article about it was written in the* Benderville Times.*)*

REVISIT THE BOOK

READER RESPONSE

1. Beginning: self-absorbed and proud, Examples: he was hostile at the karate studio, he insulted others at the book club. End: helpful and less proud, Examples: he serves the elderly, he jokes about *Hamlet.*
2. Answers will vary but may include some reference to volunteering the students may have done. It may also refer to friends or relatives' experiences. Examples from prior knowledge will clarify the students' understanding of the text.
3. Both have to do with seeing.
4. Instead of just doing something for himself, he's helping other people.

EXTEND UNDERSTANDING Have students compare the illustration on page 26 to the photo on page 28. How are they similar? How are they different? Ask students what information they learn from the caption to the photo on page 28. Ask: How does this information add to your understanding of the story?

RESPONSE OPTIONS

WRITING Invite students to write two paragraphs about the theme of this selection. They can use the notes they jotted down as they read. Encourage them to write one sentence expressing the story's "big idea." Have them support their idea with evidence from the story.

SCIENCE CONNECTION

Students can learn more about what volunteers do by going to the library or using the Internet. Suggest they research volunteer activities that clean up the environment or work with seniors. Have them find out about volunteer activities in their region and report their findings to the class.

Skill Work

TEACH/REVIEW VOCABULARY

Have students read the ninth paragraph on page 10 and explain the meaning of the word *pondered*. Ask: What word with a similar meaning could be used in place of *pondered?* Talk about the subtle difference in meaning between synonyms. Continue in a similar fashion with the remaining vocabulary words.

TARGET SKILL AND STRATEGY

PLOT AND CHARACTER Remind students that *plot* is the pattern of events in a story. Remind them that *characters* are the people in stories. Readers learn about characters through their words and actions. Encourage students as they read to jot down notes about the different characters and plot events in the book.

PRIOR KNOWLEDGE Remind students that *prior knowledge* is what a reader knows about a given topic, gathered from reading and from personal experience. Invite students to think about their knowledge of senior citizens. Ask: What have they done all their lives? What are some problems people have when they get older? Who might help older people? Have students think about what the characters in the book might do.

ELL Have students perform skits to show what they know about older people in their families or the community. What did these people do in their lives? How might they need help? How might volunteers be able to help them? Have the students perform their skits for the class.

ADDITIONAL SKILL INSTRUCTION

THEME Remind students that the *theme* is the "big idea" of a story. A statement of theme does not mention specific characters or events. Sometimes, authors state their themes for the reader. Other times, readers must infer the theme from story clues. Encourage students to jot down notes about the story's theme as they read. Remind them to be prepared to support their ideas with evidence from the story.

Plot and Character

- The **plot** is a pattern of events usually organized around a problem or conflict.

- A **character** is a person who takes part in the events of a story. Readers can learn about characters by paying attention to how they react to what happens in the story or by noting the actions they take.

Directions Fill in the graphic organizer below.

Title _____

Main Characters

Setting

Problem

Plot

_____

_____

_____

_____

_____

_____

Solution

Vocabulary

Directions Choose a word from the box to complete the chart.

Check the Words You Know			
___pondered	___putter	___recruit	___retirement

Root Word	Word	Definition
1. *retirer*, which means "to draw"		withdrawal from occupation or active working life
2. *pote*, which means "to poke"		to move or act aimlessly or idly
3. *ponderare*, which means "to weigh"		thought about, reflected on
4. *recrue*, which means "fresh growth"		to fill up with new members

Directions Read each sentence. Choose a word from the box to complete each sentence. Words may be used more than once.

5. Bill was surprised by the changes that _____ brought.

6. He _____ the best route to take to arrive at his destination.

7. With no job to fill his days, Bob had plenty of time to _____ around.

8. Herb said he would _____ and train volunteers.

9. Later, Bill _____ the success of the Sandwich Brigade.

10. Before he started helping others, he was not enjoying his _____.

Space Travel Inventions

SUMMARY Many modern-day inventions initially developed for space travel have led to new products and tools that we use in everyday life.

LESSON VOCABULARY

absorb	friction
impacts	insulation
perilous	relics
shuttle	transmitter

INTRODUCE THE BOOK

INTRODUCE THE TITLE AND AUTHOR Discuss with students the title and the author of *Space Travel Inventions*. Based on the title, ask students to say what they think the book will be about.

BUILD BACKGROUND Discuss what students know about the kinds of technology that are used in space. Ask them to think about the needs of astronauts in space. Invite them to share their thoughts about the difficulties of living in a space station.

PREVIEW/USE TEXT FEATURES As students preview the book, the photos will probably attract their attention. Suggest that students also notice captions and heads. Point out the list on page 23.

READ THE BOOK

SET PURPOSE Have students set a purpose for reading *Space Travel Inventions*. Students' interest in space exploration should guide this purpose. Suggest that students think about the most modern kinds of technology that astronauts might need on extended space flights. Or invite them to think of common modern household appliances. Ask: Which ones do you think might have been developed from space technology?

STRATEGY SUPPORT: INFERRING Remind students that when they use facts and details in a story to make a guess about something the author didn't mention, they are *inferring*. As students read *Space Travel Inventions*, encourage them to use the text and illustrations to make inferences.

COMPREHENSION QUESTIONS

PAGE 4 What tool did NASA invent to help astronauts get samples from below the moon's surface? *(cordless drill)*

PAGE 7 What was the first major sporting event to be shown live around the world? *(1964 Olympic Games in Tokyo, Japan)*

PAGE 12 How have firefighters benefited from the space program? *(Their breathing system is based on the system that astronauts used on the moon.)*

PAGE 14 What did the Federal Aviation Administration and NASA work together to develop? *(a warning system to predict wind shear used by all airlines today)*

PAGE 18 What did NASA create for the National Archives? *(an imaging device to tell the state of very old documents)*

PAGE 21 What technology has NASA developed to help clean up oil spills? *(balls of beeswax that absorb oil but not water)*

REVISIT THE BOOK

READER RESPONSE

1. The map on page 6 shows how television signals are sent by Telstar I. Responses will vary but students should specify inventions listed in the selection.
2. Possible response: I think NASA enjoys sharing information because it can inspire other ideas. This helps me understand why NASA collaborates with other companies so much.
3. Paragraphs will vary but should show students' understanding of glossary words.
4. Responses will vary but should show students' understanding of one invention and have specific reasons for their choice.

EXTEND UNDERSTANDING As students look at the photo on pages 16–17, ask how they think doctors use digital imaging to help patients. Ask if they have seen digital images from space. Have them talk about other ways digital imaging might be used.

RESPONSE OPTIONS

WRITING Suggest that students write two paragraphs about how inventions developed for space exploration have been adapted to daily life on Earth.

SCIENCE CONNECTION

Students can learn more about digital imaging on the Internet or at the library. Suggest they find a digital image of their local area as seen from space: http://images.jsc.nasa.gov/. They might also want to take a look at NASA's digital images of the solar system.

Skill Work

TEACH/REVIEW VOCABULARY

To reinforce the meaning of *perilous*, read the first paragraph on page 12. Ask students to say what they think *perilous* means. If they are not sure, have them look up the word in a dictionary. Continue in a similar fashion with the remaining vocabulary words.

TARGET SKILL AND STRATEGY

GRAPHIC SOURCES Review with students that a *graphic source* is a way of showing information visually. Some examples are graphs, maps, photographs, and diagrams. Explain that graphic sources shed light on topics that might be confusing or less interesting without graphics. Have students preview the book and note any graphic sources they see.

INFERRING Remind students that *inferring* means to make a guess from evidence and reasoning in the text rather than from direct statements from the author. After students read *Space Travel Inventions*, have them share any inferences they were able to make about the text. Have them explain how these inferences helped them understand the passage better.

ELL Have students dictate three questions about the selection to other students. Have them work together to find the answers to the questions in the book. Then have them present their questions and answers in pairs.

ADDITIONAL SKILL INSTRUCTION

GENERALIZE Remind students that a *generalization* is a broad statement that applies to many examples. It may be stated positively, as in *Many inventions from space have been adapted for domestic use.* Or it may be stated negatively, as in *No astronauts have yet explored Jupiter on foot.* Encourage students to look for clue words (*most, many, none, never,* etc.) as they try to identify the author's generalizations and formulate their own.

Graphic Sources

- **Graphic sources** are graphs, maps, pictures, photographs, charts, and diagrams that help strengthen one's understanding of the text.

Directions Use the graphic sources in *Space Travel Inventions* to answer the questions below.

1. Look at the map on page 6. Which countries and cities did the Telstar 1 transmit between?

_____

_____

2. Look at the photograph on page 8. Why do you think the roof of the stadium was constructed this way?

_____

_____

3. What is the caption on page 17 comparing? How does the photograph improve your understanding?

_____

_____

4. Look at the photograph on page 19. How does this picture of the Dead Sea Scroll improve your understanding of the text?

_____

_____

Name_____

Vocabulary

Directions Read each sentence. Write the word from the box that has the same meaning as the underlined word or phrase.

> ### Check the Words You Know
>
> ___absorb   ___friction   ___impacts   ___insulation
> ___perilous   ___relics   ___shuttle   ___transmitter

1. Special fabrics can reduce <u>the force or rubbing that slows a body in motion</u>, allowing runners or other athletes to move more swiftly.

   _____

2. The astronaut used a <u>device that sends out signals</u> to keep in contact with her fellow astronauts.

   _____

3. Foam rubber inside your helmet will <u>take in</u> the shock if you should fall and hit your head.

   _____

4. The space travelers took the <u>vehicle that runs back and forth</u> from Earth to the moon.

   _____

5. The sudden <u>jarring of objects hitting each other</u> caused the astronauts to bounce around inside the space capsule.

   _____

6. The archaeologists found many <u>objects from the past</u> at their newest digging site.

   _____

7. Astronauts face a <u>dangerous</u> adventure each time they blast off.

   _____

8. In planning the new space craft, the scientists wanted the very best <u>material for holding in heat</u> that they could find.

   _____

Directions Write a paragraph summary of *Inventions from Space Travel*. Use as many vocabulary words as you can.

_____

_____

_____

Astronauts and Cosmonauts

SUMMARY During the Cold War, the former Soviet Union and the United States competed to launch the first satellite in space. The Soviet cosmonauts won the race in the early stages, which prompted the creation of NASA and years of space exploration driven by international competition. Today, scientists from many different countries live on the *International Space Station* and cooperate in their efforts to further explore space.

LESSON VOCABULARY

aerospace   beleaguered
capsule   dissolved
germinate   gravity
rendezvous   simulator
strenuous

INTRODUCE THE BOOK

INTRODUCE THE TITLE AND AUTHOR Discuss with students the title and author of *Astronauts and Cosmonauts*. Discuss what students can predict about the article based on the title and the Science content triangle.

BUILD BACKGROUND Invite students to discuss what they know about space travel. Ask: Do you think the images you have of space travel are realistic? Remind students that we speak of Russia today because the Soviet Union collapsed in 1990. If students are unfamiliar with the topic, show a few images of American and Soviet space explorers, as well as images of the collapse of the Berlin Wall.

PREVIEW/USE TEXT FEATURES Have students go over the photos and captions before reading the text. Ask: What do the photos add? Would illustrations have worked as well? Do photos seem more scientific? Why or why not? Point out that the photos generally follow a chronological order. Ask: Does this help you predict how the article is organized?

READ THE BOOK

SET PURPOSE Guide students to set their own purposes for reading the selection. Students' interest in space travel, astronomy or other branches of science, or Cold War history should guide this purpose. Invite them to use the pictures to come up with questions they would like to have answered, such as *What was the Apollo-Soyez Mission? What do astronauts and cosmonauts do on space stations?*

STRATEGY SUPPORT: MONITOR AND FIX UP Encourage students to jot down any points that confuse them as they read. Suggest that they reread, read the surrounding text to understand context, or seek clarification from an outside source, such as a dictionary, the Internet, or a teacher.

COMPREHENSION QUESTIONS

PAGE 3 This page, unlike the pages that follow, has no bold heading. What does this suggest about the text on this page? *(Possible response: It is an introduction to the article.)*

PAGES 6–7 What is one difference between the training of astronauts and cosmonauts? *(Possible response: astronauts used "hands on" situations using simulators; cosmonauts relied on pencil-and-paper training)*

PAGES 10 AND 12 Based on these pages, which country won the early race to explore space? *(the Soviet Union)*

PAGE 21 What sentence on this page best summarizes the current state of space explanation? *(People of all nations have come together to learn and experiment as we humans look for ways to live among the stars.)*

REVISIT THE BOOK

READER RESPONSE

1. Possible response: to compare the history of space travel by Americans and Russians and to inform about what it takes to be an astronaut or cosmonaut
2. Astronauts: healthy diet, educated in "hands-on" situations; Cosmonauts: strict diet, structured physical training; Both: strenuous exercise, expected to be fit.
3. gravity: seriousness or critical
   Possible sentence: The gravity of the situation was increased when the sand bags could not contain the flood waters.
4. Responses will vary.

EXTEND UNDERSTANDING Invite students to create their own graphic device that relates information from the article, such as a time line or a chart comparing the histories of American and Russian space travel. Suggest they mark American dates in one color on the time line and Russian dates in another color.

RESPONSE OPTIONS

WRITING Ask students to imagine participating in one of the shared Russian-American meals during the *Apollo-Soyuz* mission. Have them write a brief description of their experience, including what gifts the scientists gave each other, what they ate, and what they discussed over dinner.

SCIENCE CONNECTION

Have students research a current science project overseen by NASA. Suggest they use NASA's official Website: www. nasa.gov. Ask them to present a brief summary of this project.

Skill Work

TEACH/REVIEW VOCABULARY

Ask students to create a word web for each vocabulary word, with the word itself in the center and all associated words forming outer circles of the web.

ELL Divide students into groups and ask each group to use pictures or gestures to express the meaning of each vocabulary word.

TARGET SKILL AND STRATEGY

AUTHOR'S PURPOSE Tell students that an *author's purpose* is the reason or reasons that she or he has for writing. (persuade, inform, entertain, or express) Remind students that they must often infer the author's purpose from text clues. *Astronauts and Cosmonauts*, for example, contains dates, historic photos, and many facts about the history of space travel.
Ask: What does this suggest about the author's purpose?

MONITOR AND FIX UP Tell students that *monitoring* and *fixing up* is the process by which they keep track of their own comprehension. Remind them to notice if the text stops making sense and to ask themselves questions such as *What does this mean?* and *Why did the author include this?* Answering such questions will also help students identify the author's purpose.

ADDITIONAL SKILL INSTRUCTION

COMPARE AND CONTRAST Remind students that *comparing* and *contrasting* means noting similarities and differences between things. Point out that authors sometimes employ clue words or phrases *(like, unlike, however, on the other hand)* when comparing and contrasting. Help students see that *Astronauts and Cosmonauts*, beginning with the title, is a comparison of Russian and American space exploration. Suggest students make a Venn diagram to compare and contrast the article's information.

Author's Purpose

- An **author's purpose** is the reason or reasons an author has for writing.
- Four common reasons are: **to persuade, to inform, to entertain, to express ideas.**

Directions Read the paragraphs below. Then answer the questions on the lines below.

> From the beginning of time, people have stared at the stars in wonder. Their beauty and mystery has always attracted people.
>
> In the late 1950s, the United States and the former Soviet Union started working to get a closer look at the stars. Each wanted to send people into space. At the time, the two countries were not friendly and competed to be the first in space. Each kept their work top secret.

1. What would you say is the author's main purpose in writing the first paragraph?

_____

2. Explain your answer.

_____

_____

3. What purpose might the author have in the second paragraph?

_____

4. Explain your answer.

_____

_____

5. How do you think the author's two purposes might work together?

_____

_____

Vocabulary

Directions Write the word from the box that belongs in each group.

Check the Words You Know

___aerospace	___beleagurered	___capsule
___dissolved	___germinate	___gravity
___rendezvous	___simulator	___strenuous

1. meet, gather, _____

2. force, pull, _____

3. difficult, exhausting, _____

4. worried, troubled, _____

5. apparatus, device, _____

6. sprout, grow, _____

7. flight, space, _____

8. rocket, front section, _____

9. broken up, ended, _____

Directions Write two sentences on the lines below about Astronauts and Cosmonauts. Use as many vocabulary words as you can.

_____

_____

_____

_____

_____

_____

The Shaping of the Continents

SUMMARY The planet Earth today consists of seven continents separated by the world's oceans. Evidence suggests, however, that hundreds of millions of years ago, the continents were all connected. This book explains plate tectonics, the force that moves continents, and the ways that mountains are formed.

LESSON VOCABULARY

converge	diverge
fossils	magma
plastic	subduction
supercontinent	unconventional

INTRODUCE THE BOOK

INTRODUCE THE TITLE AND AUTHOR Discuss with students the title and the author of *The Shaping of the Continents.* Based on the title, ask students what they think the book will be about. Ask them what they think the title means.

BUILD BACKGROUND Discuss what students know about how the continents were formed. Ask: Were the continents always in the same place? What forces might move continents? Ask them what they know about the causes of earthquakes and how mountains are formed.

PREVIEW/USE TEXT FEATURES As students preview the book, have them notice the section heads, maps, photographs, and diagrams. Ask them how they think these text features complement the text in this selection.

READ THE BOOK

SET PURPOSE Have students set a purpose for reading *The Shaping of the Continents.* Students' interest in the history of the Earth and the scientists who study the Earth should guide this purpose. Suggest that students jot down notes about their purpose as they read.

STRATEGY SUPPORT: SUMMARIZE As students read, suggest they summarize the main idea in each section. Remind them to write only about the most important ideas and leave out less-important details. Students may later want to combine their section summaries and create a comprehensive summary of the selection.

COMPREHENSION QUESTIONS

PAGE 4 What is the meaning of *Pangaea*? *(all lands)*

PAGE 5 What is the name for the theory that explains how the continents shift and move? *(continental drift)*

PAGE 6 What made Alfred Wegener believe that South America and Africa might once have been connected? *(They had matching coastlines that contained the same plant and animal fossils and similar rock and land formations.)*

PAGE 7 What caused scientists in the 1950s to change their understanding of how the Earth's surface moves? *(They discovered that the ocean floor spreads, making the ocean wider and moving the surrounding continents farther apart.)*

PAGE 13 What happens when an ocean floor pushes toward a landmass? Why? *(The ocean floor will always slide under the landmass because the landmass is less dense.)*

REVISIT THE BOOK

READER RESPONSE

1. Possible responses: Divergent Plates: Effect: The spreading sea floor pushes the tectonic plates, and the plates and landmasses that ride on them, apart; Convergent Plates: Cause: Two plates crash into each other; Effect: An earthquake is triggered.
2. Possible response: The parts of the large landmass moved on the Earth's surface until there were seven continents.
3. Possible response: They are opposite. *con-:* with, together; *di-:* two; Can you *conceal* the stain? I tried to *divert* his attention.
4. Responses will vary.

EXTEND UNDERSTANDING Have students look at the text and art on page 11 showing diagrams of convergent and divergent plate movement. Ask students how the images convey information in a way that complements the information in the text. Ask: What do the diagrams show you about plate movement?

RESPONSE OPTIONS

WRITING Invite students to write two paragraphs about causes and effects they learned about in this selection. They can use the notes they jotted down as they read the book. Encourage them to use clue words such as *since, thus, as a result, therefore,* and *consequently* to show relationships between what happened and why it happened.

SCIENCE CONNECTION

Students can learn more about plate tectonics on the Internet or at the library. Suggest they find out about significant earthquakes such as the underwater quake that was responsible for the tsunami in the Indian Ocean or the eruption of Mount St. Helens in Washington State. Have them report their findings to the class.

Skill Work

TEACH/REVIEW VOCABULARY

Form pairs of students. Then have each student write a cloze sentence for each vocabulary word on separate cards. Have partners exchange cards and take turns completing each sentence with the correct vocabulary word.

TARGET SKILL AND STRATEGY

CAUSE AND EFFECT Remind students that a *cause* is why something happened. An *effect* is what happened. Introduce clue words such as *since, thus, as a result, therefore,* and *consequently.* Explain that these words indicate a relationship between why something happened and what happened. Encourage students to take note of causes and effects as they read.

ELL Invite students to create two-sentence pairs using the clue words *since, thus, as a result, therefore,* and *consequently.* Explain that the clue words show relationships between what happened and why it happened. Make sure they use the clue words correctly to indicate cause-and-effect relationships.

SUMMARIZE Remind students that *summarizing* is a strategy that good readers use to check their understanding of a selection. When you summarize, you make a brief statement that gives the main ideas of an article. Challenge students to summarize an important cause-and-effect relationship in each section.

ADDITIONAL SKILL INSTRUCTION

GRAPHIC SOURCES Remind students that *graphic sources* include charts and tables, diagrams, maps, pictures with captions, and timelines. Encourage students to think about the kinds of information provided by the graphic sources in this reader. For each graphic source, ask: What do you learn from this graphic source that you do not learn in the text?

Cause and Effect

- A **cause** is "why something happened."

- An **effect** is "what happened."

Directions Draw a line to match each cause with its effect.

Cause

1. The Earth's crust shifted.

2. The continents separated.

3. Scientists saw that the ocean floor spreads.

4. Two plates move apart, or diverge.

5. Two plates meet, and one slides under the other.

6. An ocean floor pushes toward a landmass.

7. Two landmasses meet.

8. Two plates slide past each other and get stuck.

9. Inside a volcano, trapped gases expand as they rise.

10. Tectonic plates move at a very, very slow rate.

Effect

An earthquake occurs.

Scientists developed the theory of plate tectonics.

The landmasses fold and crumple, producing mountain ranges.

Molten rock from within the mantle spews forth, creating new ocean floor.

Very deep trenches occur.

Pangaea broke into two distinct landmasses.

The ocean floor slides under the land.

We are not likely to see much change in the Earth during our lifetimes.

The volcano erupts.

Earth's one great ocean separated into smaller oceans.

Name_____

Vocabulary

Directions Choose a word from the box to complete the chart.

Check the Words You Know

___converge	___diverge
___fossils	___magma
___plastic	___subduction
___supercontinent	___unconventional

Root Word	Word	Definition
1. *sub + ducere*, which means "to draw or tow"		the process of one plate sliding underneath another plate
2. *massein*, which means "to knead"		molten rock beneath the Earth's surface
3. *dis + vergere*, which means "to incline"		to split apart from
4. *un + convenire*, which means "not + coming together"		not conforming to accepted rules or standards
5. *fossilis*, which means "obtained by digging"		remains of plants or animals that lived in the past, preserved as rock

Directions Write a paragraph about *The Shaping of the Continents*. Use the vocabulary words which were not used in the chart above.

_____

_____

_____

_____

_____

_____

_____

107

From Territory to Statehood

SUMMARY This work presents a collection of stories of western territories and the process by which they became states. It begins with a discussion of The Louisiana Purchase, Lewis and Clark's expedition, and The Missouri Compromise. The work covers the historical context of the period and touches on important social issues affecting the statehood process, such as the practice of slavery. It contains a chronological chart of all the states admitted to the United States in the 1800s.

LESSON VOCABULARY

annexed	bill
compromise	expedition
inhabited	interpreter
precedent	ratification

INTRODUCE THE BOOK

INTRODUCE THE TITLE AND AUTHOR Discuss with students the title and author of *From Territory to Statehood*. Based on the title, ask students what they think the selection will be about. Does the cover give any clues?

BUILD BACKGROUND Ask students if they know the year that their state achieved statehood. What was the most recent state of the 50 United States to achieve statehood? (*Hawaii in 1959*)

PREVIEW/USE TEXT FEATURES As students look through the book, encourage them to note the headings, photographs, pictures, and captions. Do these features give them a better sense of what the book will be about?

READ THE BOOK

SET PURPOSE Most students will be interested in reading this book so that they can learn about the history of western states. Students may focus on the history of the practice of slavery as it affected states in the western United States.

STRATEGY SUPPORT: QUESTIONING As students read, encourage them to ask questions about the text. Remind them that asking questions will allow them to test their comprehension and identify which answers they should be looking for.

COMPREHENSION QUESTIONS

PAGE 3 How many states did the United States have originally? (*thirteen*)

PAGE 4 What country did President Jefferson make a deal with in The Louisiana Purchase? (*France*)

PAGE 6 What group of people did Lewis and Clark set out to learn more about? (*Native Americans*)

PAGE 8 Which national body has to approve admission of a new state? (*Congress*)

PAGE 11 When the Missouri Compromise was reached, how many slave states and how many free states were there? (*twelve of each*)

REVISIT THE BOOK

READER RESPONSE

1. Possible response: The generalization is valid because a number of examples support it. The admissions of the Missouri, California, Kansas, and Nebraska territories were delayed over the issue of slavery.
2. Questions will vary.
3. Responses will vary but should match the definitions given or implied in the text.
4. Possible response: African Americans could still be enslaved. Native Americans were pushed out of their territory. White Americans used the new areas to further their own political beliefs and their need for land.

EXTEND UNDERSTANDING Look through the book together with students and discuss how the historical photographs and maps give an accurate picture of what life was like in the 1800s.

RESPONSE OPTIONS

WRITING Have students write a letter from the point of view of one of the Native American tribal members that Lewis and Clark met on their expedition. Have students assume they have never seen a white man before, and describe their encounter with Lewis and Clark. What did their language sound like? What did their food taste like?

SOCIAL STUDIES CONNECTION

Time For SOCIAL STUDIES

Have students pick one of the western states listed on a chart in the selection and research it on the Internet or in the library. What is unique about the history of that state before and after statehood? What are the state flower and bird?

Skill Work

TEACH/REVIEW VOCABULARY

Encourage student pairs to find the vocabulary words in the text. Have them define the words and then work together to write a sentence for each word.

ELL Invite students to look at the pictures in the book to tell in their own words what this book is about.

TARGET SKILL AND STRATEGY

GENERALIZE As this selection presents the stories of a number of different states' journeys to statehood, students will need to organize these facts in order to *generalize*. As they read the text, have them consider what these states have in common. Which of these states were originally slave states, and which were free states?

QUESTIONING Review with students that both *asking questions* and *answering questions* will improve their understanding of the text. As students read, encourage them to pause periodically to ask questions about the text. If they are unable to find the answer by rereading that portion, encourage them to read on in the text to find the answer.

ADDITIONAL SKILL INSTRUCTION

SEQUENCE Remind students that *sequence* means the order in which things happen. Have students look at the time sequence table on page 12 and answer the following questions: In what year did the most states achieve statehood? How many states achieved statehood between 1850 and 1875?

Generalize

- A **generalization** is a broad statement or rule that applies to many examples. A generalization is made after thinking about a number of examples or facts and what they have in common.
- A **valid generalization** is adequately supported by specific facts and logic.
- A **faulty generalization** is not adequately supported by facts or logic.

Directions Review *From Territory to Statehood*. Write whether each generalization below is *valid* or *faulty*.

1. _____ Part of the Corps of Discovery group's mission was to learn about Native Americans.

2. _____ All territories had to follow the same process to become states.

3. _____ In the early 1800s, all people in the South owned slaves.

4. _____ In the North in the early 1800s, it was against the law in all states to own slaves.

5. _____ Many people moved to California during the Gold Rush.

6. _____ Everyone in the North was angry about the Kansas-Nebraska Act.

7. _____ With the building of railroads across the nation, few settlers in far-off areas were within reach of cities and towns.

8. _____ The western states in our Union were settled by people who wanted a life of freedom.

Directions Write one valid and one faulty generalization of your own.

9. Valid _____

_____

10. Faulty _____

_____

Name_____

Vocabulary

Directions Fill in the blank with the word from the box that matches the definition.

> ### Check the Words You Know
>
> ___annexed   ___bill   ___compromise   ___expedition
>
> ___inhabited   ___interpreter   ___precedent   ___ratification

1. _____   *v.* lived in

2. _____   *n.* approval of a proposed constitution

3. _____   *n.* journey made for a specific purpose

4. _____   *v.* added territory to an existing city, county, state, or nation

5. _____   *n.* resolution of differences in which both sides give up something

6. _____   *n.* example used to justify later decisions

7. _____   *n.* a proposed law

8. _____   *n.* someone who helps people who speak different languages communicate with each other

Directions Complete each analogy with a word from the box.

Example: GIRL is to BOY as MOTHER is to ___FATHER___.

9. DESERTED is to CROWDED as VACANT is to _____.

10. PROBLEM is to SOLUTION as DISAGREEMENT is to _____.

11. SUBTRACTED is to DELETED as ADDED is to _____.

How the Wolves Saved Yellowstone

⊚ DRAW CONCLUSIONS
⊚ IMPORTANT IDEAS

SUMMARY In this nonfiction selection, the importance of wolves in an ecosystem is explored. Once plentiful and then nonexistent in Yellowstone National Park, wolves are returned to recreate the balance of nature needed in the park's ecosystem for all other living things to survive.

LESSON VOCABULARY

adamantly	dramatic	foragers
forum	hoarding	logical
measure	prowess	reimburse
relentlessly		

INTRODUCE THE BOOK

INTRODUCE THE TITLE AND AUTHOR Discuss the title and author of *How the Wolves Saved Yellowstone*. Ask students what they think this book will be about.

BUILD BACKGROUND Discuss what students know about wolves. Ask them how they think a wolf can save something. Explain that Yellowstone is a National Park where many different types of wildlife live. Have students think about why it might be important for wolves to live in a wildlife park.

PREVIEW/USE TEXT FEATURES After students have previewed the book, discuss how photographs can help strengthen their understanding of the text. Remind students that captions tell something about the photographs. Have students turn to page 17. Discuss the feature of a map and its key. Then, have students turn to pages 22–23. Discuss the feature of activities. Finally, remind students that the Glossary in the back of the book provides definitions of words they might not know.

READ THE BOOK

SET PURPOSE Have students set a purpose for reading *How the Wolves Saved Yellowstone*. As students read, have them list the ways that wolves help other animals.

STRATEGY SUPPORT: IMPORTANT IDEAS Remind students that, besides chapter titles and headings, important ideas can be found within the text. Read page 4 with students. Discuss the two important ideas of Yellowstone National Park and hunters killing all of the wolves. Discuss the details that support these two ideas.

COMPREHENSION QUESTIONS

PAGES 3–4 Why did wolves disappear from Yellowstone? (*People hunted them because they were afraid the wolves might kill their livestock.*)

PAGES 5–8 What conclusion can you draw from the absence of wolves in Yellowstone? What details or facts support your conclusion? (*Possible response: The absence of wolves had a devastating effect on Yellowstone National Park; increase in coyotes caused foxes and owls to starve, the deer population to go down, and an overpopulation of elk ate too much new vegetation so growth came to a halt.*)

PAGE 11 What is the important idea on this page? What details support that idea? (*Ranchers fought to keep wolves out of Yellowstone. Ranchers persuaded members of Congress to support them. Ranchers threatened to kill wolves even though it was illegal.*)

PAGES 18–20 How has the return of wolves changed the park? (*coyote population decreased; deer population increased; other animals get food from wolves' leftovers; return of native vegetation trees are growing which provides food for other animals and beaver dams*)

112   How the Wolves Saved Yellowstone

REVIST THE BOOK

READER RESPONSE

1. Responses may vary but make sure students understand the concept of drawing conclusions.
2. Responses will vary but students should list at least two important ideas that ensure they understand the concept.
3. Possible response: *Measure* means to check the amount of something. Sentences may vary but make sure students show an understanding of both meanings of *measure*.
4. Responses may vary but make sure students include an explanation.

EXTEND UNDERSTANDING Discuss the importance of the food chain. Explain that every living thing depends on other living things to survive. List the animals mentioned in the book and the food each of those animals depends on for survival. Create a food chain chart using the information gathered.

RESPONSE OPTIONS

SPEAKING Have students write a speech either promoting or blocking the return of wolves to Yellowstone National Park. Have students orally present their speech to the class.

SCIENCE CONNECTION

TIME FOR Science

Have students research other National Parks, on the Internet or at the library. Have them gather information about the wildlife and vegetation found in those parks. Students can write a report about what they learned.

Skill Work

TEACH/REVIEW VOCABULARY

Write a vocabulary word on the board. Have students brainstorm what they think the word means. Next, have students find the word in the text and use context clues to revise or add meanings to the list on the board. Then, have students look in the Glossary to check their understanding. Repeat with each vocabulary word.

ELL Have more proficient English speakers act out (Drama) the meaning of some words. As appropriate, include less proficient English speakers.

TARGET SKILL AND STRATEGY

DRAW CONCLUSIONS Remind students that a *conclusion* is a sensible decision reached after thinking about details or facts in what is read. Have students turn to page 9. Discuss the conclusion made by scientists and then the conclusion made by Aldo Leopold. Discuss the details stated in the text that support those conclusions. Then, have students turn to page 21. Point out the heading *Conclusion*. Discuss the "final" conclusion made by the author (*The Yellowstone Wolf Project has been a great success so far*) and the details in the text that support that conclusion.

IMPORTANT IDEAS Remind students that *important ideas* are the major parts or topics of a story, and are often presented in nonfiction texts through various types of graphic features. Explain that each important idea is supported by details. Discuss the headings on pages 3, 4, 8, 10, 13, 18, and 21. As students read, have them list details from the text that support these important ideas.

ADDITIONAL SKILL INSTRUCTION

MAIN IDEA AND DETAILS Remind students that the *main idea* is the most important idea about a topic. *Supporting details* are pieces of information that tell more about the main idea. Explain that sometimes a main idea can come from the title of a book. After reading, discuss the details from the book that support "How the Wolves Saved Yellowstone" as the main idea.

Draw Conclusions

- **Drawing Conclusions** means to make sensible decisions after thinking about details or facts in what you read.

Directions Read the excerpt from *How the Wolves Saved Yellowstone*. Then answer the questions that follow.

> A biologist named Renee Askins came to the aid of the government. An avid wolf supporter, she began a campaign in 1981 to win over the ranchers who adamantly objected to the Yellowstone plan. She traveled throughout the west, speaking to groups of ranchers, explaining that wolves in balanced ecosystems actually killed very few cows and sheep.
>
> Additional help came from an organization that protected wildlife. They raised money in order to reimburse any ranchers for livestock that might be lost to wolves. Even so, some ranchers still objected to the plan.
>
> Finally, the government agreed that ranchers would be allowed to shoot and kill any Yellowstone wolves that attacked their livestock. This satisfied the ranchers, and by 1994— more than a dozen years after Askins began her campaign—many of the ranchers who had objected to the Yellowstone wolf plan were now willing to accept it.

1. What conclusion can you draw about Renee Askins' role in the Yellowstone plan?

_____

_____

2. Give at least one detail or fact that supports your conclusion.

_____

_____

3. What conclusion can you draw about the change in the ranchers' attitude?

_____

_____

4. Give at least two details or facts that support your conclusion.

_____

_____

Vocabulary

Directions For each vocabulary word listed below, circle the two words that have the *same* meaning.

> ### Check the Words You Know
>
> ___adamantly   ___dramatic   ___foragers
> ___forum   ___hoarding   ___logical
> ___measure   ___prowess   ___reimburse
> ___relentlessly

1. adamantly	rigidly	willingly	obstinately	reasonably
2. dramatic	theatrical	emotional	monotonous	shy
3. foragers	sitters	watchers	searchers	grazers
4. forum	room	conference	powwow	building
5. hoarding	storing	sharing	stashing	spending
6. logical	unreasonable	reasonable	invalid	valid
7. measure	scale	limit	tape	length
8. reimburse	take	refund	repay	give
9. relentlessly	unyieldingly	softly	weakly	determinedly

Directions Write the definition for *prowess*.

10. _____

Mixed-Up Vegetables

SUMMARY This book examines genetic engineering as it applies to food. Many people believe that altering food can help to solve the world's food shortage. Other people believe that altering food is dangerous and could bring harm to people and the Earth. The book shows how farmers and scientists have changed vegetables and the reasons for such changes.

LESSON VOCABULARY

beneficial	gene
genetically altered	pesticides
transgenic organisms	

INTRODUCE THE BOOK

INTRODUCE THE TITLE AND AUTHOR Discuss with students the title and author of *Mixed-Up Vegetables*. Based on the title and the cover photograph, ask students to describe what they imagine this book will be about.

BUILD BACKGROUND Ask students to discuss the vegetables and fruits they like the best. If they could change them, what sorts of changes would they like to see? Is there a particular fruit they enjoy that doesn't grow locally? Have students heard about genetic engineering? Do they understand how genetics work in people? Have them talk about what they understand about genetics.

PREVIEW/USE TEXT FEATURES Have students look at the section headings and the photographs and discuss how these text elements help to organize the book. Ask students how the section headings may help them understand what the book may be about.

READ THE BOOK

SET PURPOSE Have students set a purpose for reading *Mixed-Up Vegetables*. Students' curiosity about vegetables and genetic engineering can guide this purpose. Since this book presents many contrasting opinions, students can decide which side of the argument they support.

STRATEGY SUPPORT: TEXT STRUCTURE Encourage students to identify the book's external text structure, as evident in the title, headings, paragraphs, charts, graphs, photos, and the like. Then ask them to think about the way the text is internally structured, i.e., the logical connections between ideas. Guide students to see that *Mixed-Up Vegetables* is internally structured by comparing and contrasting the two main views on genetic engineering (for or against).

COMPREHENSION QUESTIONS

PAGE 3 What resulted when a gene from a cold water fish was inserted into genes for a tomato plant? *(A tomato resulted that could grow in colder weather than other tomatoes.)*

PAGE 5 Other than genetic alteration through experiments, what are two ways that farmers have used for changing plants? *(selective breeding and grafting)*

PAGE 7 What do you call plants or other organisms that have had their genetic makeup altered? *(transgenic organisms)*

PAGE 11 Nonmodified tomatoes are picked when they are what color? *(green)*

PAGE 15 Do transgenic vegetables have to be labeled as such? *(no)*

PAGE 16 Why can it be a problem when scientists develop insect-resistant crops? *(Some insects develop a resistance to the plants, making them more dangerous.)*

REVISIT THE BOOK

READER RESPONSE

1. Possible response: Detail: Pests can become resistant to genetically altered poisons. Detail: Transgenic plants can be a danger to other wildlife. Detail: Transgenic vegetables can cause allergies. Main Idea: Some people believe that genetic alteration of vegetables is a mistake.

2. The headings are questions that provide a purpose for reading. Possible outline for page 5:
   I. Plant alteration is not a new idea.
      A. Selective breeding has been used for years.
      B. Grafting has been used for years.

3. *genetic:* having to do with origin and natural growth; *genetically:* in a way that involves genes; *transgenic:* having altered genes.

4. Responses will vary, but students should support their answers.

EXTEND UNDERSTANDING Discuss with students how sections in books can help organize complicated material. Go over all the boldface heads with students and discuss what material is in each section and why. Ask students how they can tell what each section is going to be about. Help them see that each successive section is a progression.

RESPONSE OPTIONS

WRITING Have students write a paragraph in defense of genetic engineering of food or against it. Have them use some of the details from the book to support their case. Ask them to consider who benefits from such genetic manipulation or who is harmed by it.

SCIENCE CONNECTION

Have students research the Flavr Savr tomato on the Internet or at the library. Students should try to find out as much as they can about the development of this new tomato. They should check at their local supermarket to see if that brand of tomato is available. Ask the grocer if any of the genetically modified foods are marked as such. Can seeds for this tomato be bought at the local nursery?

Skill Work

TEACH/REVIEW VOCABULARY

To reinforce the contextual meaning of the word *beneficial* on page 4, discuss with students how the phrase *allows farmers to grow much more* helps to guess the meaning of *beneficial.* Repeat this exercise with the rest of the vocabulary words in the book.

ELL Ask English language learners to skim the article and write down any unfamiliar words. Suggest they look the words up in the dictionary and write the meaning in their notebooks.

TARGET SKILL AND STRATEGY

MAIN IDEA AND DETAILS Remind students that each text can be boiled down to a number of *main ideas.* Remind students that each of the main ideas will be supported by a number of supporting *details.* As they read this text, have them take a piece of paper and write down what the main ideas are. Then have them list next to each main idea the details that support it.

TEXT STRUCTURE Remind students that authors use different *text structures* to help readers pay attention to certain details about the topic. Point out to students that most of the section headings in this book are phrased as questions. Ask: Why did the author structure the text in this way? Does each section have a main idea?

ADDITIONAL SKILL INSTRUCTION

COMPARE AND CONTRAST Remind students that when we *compare* two things we examine how they are alike, and when we *contrast* two things we examine how they are different. In this text, the author often contrasts the thoughts of people who are for genetic engineering with the thoughts of people who are against it. Have students pay attention to these contrasting opinions as they read the text.

Main Idea and Details

- The **main idea** is the most important idea about a topic.
- Supporting **details** are small pieces of information that tell more about the main idea.

Directions Use the diagram below to write the main idea and supporting details of *Mixed-Up Vegetables*. Write the main idea in the center.

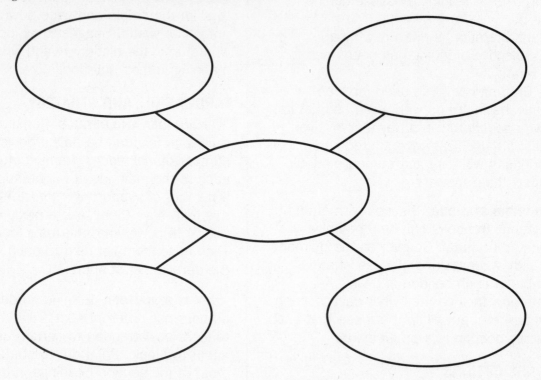

Directions Look at the chart on page 8. In the center of the diagram below, write the main idea for the chart. Add four details that support the main idea.

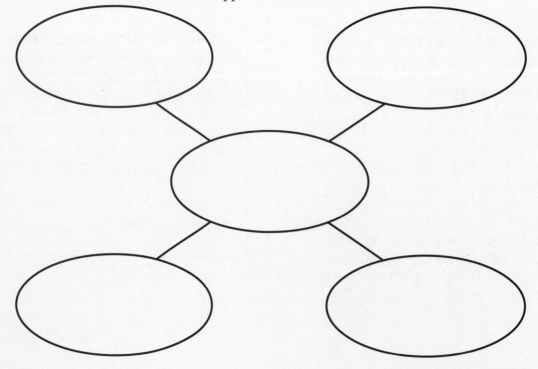

Name_____

Vocabulary

Directions Write the vocabulary word that matches each definition.

1. chemicals sprayed on crops to kill insects _____

2. contains genes that have been artificially inserted _____

3. a tiny unit that tells what a living thing will look like _____

4. something good or useful _____

5. genes that have been added to plants or animals to make changes _____

Directions Write a paragraph discussing the risks of genetically engineered vegetables as described in *Mixed-Up Vegetables,* using as many vocabulary words as possible.

_____

_____

_____

_____

_____

_____

_____

_____

_____

_____

Precious Goods: From Salt to Silk

SUMMARY This nonfiction selection explores the history of salt, silk, gold, diamonds, and oil. Obtaining and trading such precious goods has had both good and bad consequences, such as spreading ideas across cultures and starting wars.

LESSON VOCABULARY

commodities	excavating
luster	malleable
microorganisms	molten
preserve	synthetic

INTRODUCE THE BOOK

INTRODUCE THE TITLE AND AUTHOR Discuss with students the title and authors of *Precious Goods: From Salt to Silk*. Draw students' attention to the cover photo. Ask: What do you think this selection will be about? The content triangle says *Social Studies*; what does that suggest?

BUILD BACKGROUND Discuss with students what they already know about the history of precious goods such as gold or oil. Ask students what news they have recently heard, for example, about oil prices. Ask: Have any of you seen an oil field, or pictures in the news of an oil field? What are some of the uses of oil today? Why is oil sometimes called *black gold*?

PREVIEW/USE TEXT FEATURES Have students read the title and spend a few minutes looking at the photos, graphs, and maps. Discuss what these suggest about the selection's content. Draw students' attention, for example, to the graph on page 19 and ask them to discuss what this tells them about oil use in the world.

READ THE BOOK

SET PURPOSE Guide students to set their own purposes for reading the selection. Students' interest in history or in a precious item such as gold should guide this purpose. Suggest that students imagine an item they value that is scarce or hard for them to obtain.

STRATEGY SUPPORT: TEXT STRUCTURE Preview the external text structure with students. Have them call out different ways the authors have organized the text. *(headings, bullets)* As students read the text, call attention to the internal text structure. Ask: Is there a pattern to the headings and their sections? Guide students in understanding that the headings present important ideas and the text in the sections present details.

COMPREHENSION QUESTIONS

PAGE 3 What is one common factor that makes salt, silk, gold, diamonds, and oil precious? *(At one time, they were all scarce or hard to obtain.)*

PAGES 10–11 What was one good result of the silk trade? *(China became linked to Europe, and ideas were traded between cultures.)*

PAGES 9 AND 18 How is the history of silk similar to the history of diamonds? *(Silk and diamonds were each exclusive to one country for centuries.)*

PAGE 21 What do you think will happen if most countries continue to meet their energy needs with oil? *(The struggle for oil control will continue.)*

REVISIT THE BOOK

READER RESPONSE

1. Possible response: Silk: fabric woven from thread of silkworm's cocoon, no longer a precious commodity; Diamonds: crystal made of carbon, still a precious commodity; Both: exclusive to one country for centuries

2. Possible response: The headings gave me a clue as to what the section would mostly be about.

3. *Harmless* means "without harm," while *harmful* means "full of harm;" *worthless(ness), spoonful, beautiful, skillful(ly), colorless;* definitions will vary.

4. Responses will vary but should include reasons.

EXTEND UNDERSTANDING Ask students to look at each of the regional maps in the article. Then present either a world map or a globe so that students can see where these regions lie in relation to each other and have a global picture of the various trade routes discussed in the article.

RESPONSE OPTIONS

WRITING Have students reread pages 20-21. Then ask them to write a summary of the information in the text and in the graph.

SOCIAL STUDIES CONNECTION

Time For **SOCIAL STUDIES**

Ask students to research oil production in the countries of the Persian Gulf on the Internet or at the library. Have them look at the amount of oil produced in each country, the daily prices and how these affect gas prices locally, and what political issues arise. Encourage students to share their research.

Skill Work

TEACH/REVIEW VOCABULARY

Reinforce comprehension by challenging students to write sentences that use two or more of the vocabulary words. Hold a contest to see if anyone can combine all the vocabulary words in one sentence.

ELL Invite students to look at the pictures in the book to tell in their own words what the book is about.

TARGET SKILL AND STRATEGY

COMPARE AND CONTRAST Remind students that to *compare* and *contrast* is to look for similarities and differences between two objects, ideas, or pieces of text. Draw students' attention to the heads reading *The Value of Salt, The Value of Silk,* and so on. Point out that the authors have organized the entire text to underline the similarities and differences among the precious goods.

TEXT STRUCTURE Remind students that *text structure* is the way an author has organized nonfiction text. Have students work in pairs to use the headings in the book to construct multiple Web graphic organizers. Then have them use the information in each section to fill in the outer circles of their Webs. Have students explain how this graphic organizer helps them understand the content of the book.

ADDITIONAL SKILL INSTRUCTION

DRAW CONCLUSIONS Remind students that *drawing a conclusion* means making a sensible decision or forming a reasonable opinion after thinking about the facts and details in what they have read. Drawing conclusions helps students synthesize what they have read, draw on their own life experiences, and identify an author's purpose. Suggest that students make a list of key facts in this selection and use them to come to a reasonable conclusion.

Compare and Contrast

- To **compare** is to tell how two or more things are alike. Authors may use clue words and phrases such as *similar to, like,* or *as* to compare.
- To **contrast** is to tell how two or more things are different. Authors may use clue words such as *different from, but, unlike, on the other hand,* or *however* to contrast.

Directions Read the passage below. Then compare and contrast the results of the desire for these precious goods. How are the results similar throughout history and across the range of goods? How are they different or specific to that particular item? Use the chart at the bottom of the page to organize your answers.

Over 1,000 years ago, West African realms became rich by selling salt, as they were near salt mines. They had the endless supplies of salt that the Europeans wanted. Traders started trade routes from the salt mines in the Sahara desert to the Mediterranean Sea.

Similarly, Persian traders became very rich selling silk. They could ask any price they wanted for the precious fabric, which only the Chinese knew how to produce. Silk makers guarded their secret carefully for about 3,000 years. Traders carried their goods 5,000 miles across Asia on routes that together were known as the Silk Road. Ideas were traded along with the silk and other goods. The desire for silk was important in linking Europe to China.

Over 2,000 years ago, African invaders entered Spain to take possession of its gold. The invaders became rich, and many Spanish people were forced to mine gold. In North America of the 1840s, news of gold attracted thousands of gold diggers. The area grew so quickly that California applied for statehood.

Diamonds have long been considered precious. Today, armies that control diamond-rich sections of their countries use "conflict diamonds" to pay for their wars.

The desire for oil, most of which is in the Middle East, has also led to military conflict and international struggles to control oil resources.

Results of Desire for Precious Goods

Alike	**Different**

Vocabulary

Directions Write the vocabulary word that matches each definition.

> ## Check the Words You Know
>
> ___commodities ___excavating ___luster ___malleable
> ___microorganisms ___molten ___preserve ___synthetic

1. _____ *adj.* able to be shaped or formed as by hammering or pressure

2. _____ *n.* any things that are bought and sold

3. _____ *n.* soft reflected light; sheen

4. _____ *adj.* made liquid by heat; melted

5. _____ *v.* exposing or uncovering by digging out, as a mine

6. _____ *adj.* created by humans rather than found in nature; artificial

7. _____ *n.* organisms so small that they can only be seen with a microscope, such as bacteria

8. _____ *v.* to prevent something, such as food, from decaying or spoiling

Directions Write a brief paragraph about one precious commodity listed in *Precious Goods: From Salt to Silk*. Use as many vocabulary words as possible.

_____

_____

_____

_____

_____

_____

_____

_____

Traveling by Plane

SUMMARY Join the García family, 21st century travelers, as they take a plane from Chicago to Denver. Grandma reflects on how—from ticketing to checking in to in-flight entertainment—flying has come a long way. This book talks about the future of commercial space flight as well.

LESSON VOCABULARY

agent	altitude
confiscate	cruising
kiosk	tarmac
taxis	turbulence

INTRODUCE THE BOOK

INTRODUCE THE TITLE AND AUTHOR Discuss with students the title and author of *Traveling by Plane.* Invite students to say what this book might be about, based on the title.

BUILD BACKGROUND Discuss what students know about the early history of airplanes. Ask if they know the names of the inventors of the first aircraft (Wilbur and Orville Wright). Ask how air travel today is different than it was twenty years ago.

PREVIEW/USE TEXT FEATURES Invite students to preview the book by looking at heads, maps, photos, and captions. Ask them to consider how these features add to the book. Invite them to say why they think the map on pages 12–13 is included. Ask: What are time zones?

READ THE BOOK

SET PURPOSE Guide students to set their own purposes for reading the selection. Students' interest in airplanes and the history of flight should guide this purpose. Invite them to consider how airplane travel has changed over the years and how it might still change in the years to come.

STRATEGY SUPPORT: PREDICT AND SET PURPOSE
Remind students that to *predict* means to tell what you think might happen next in a story or article based on what you have already read. As students read *Traveling by Plane,* encourage them to make predictions about the text. Then have them continue reading for the purpose of confirming or revising their predictions.

ELL Invite more proficient peers to work with less proficient peers to record their questions or help them formulate their questions. They may wish to use a graphic organizer to record their questions before, during, and after reading the book.

COMPREHENSION QUESTIONS

PAGE 3 How did the Wright brothers reward Charley Furnas? What did they reward him for? *(by making him the first American air passenger; for helping them in his spare time)*

PAGE 5 What are e-tickets? *(electronic tickets issued by the airline and created online)*

PAGE 10 What is one way commercial air travel today is different from earlier times? *(much of the navigation is automated)*

PAGE 13 In addition to monitoring the electronic tracking system, what do air traffic controllers do before giving the final clearance to land? *(They scan the sky and runways with binoculars.)*

PAGE 16 "Computers will likely play an even bigger role in future air travel." Is this a statement of fact or of opinion? Explain. *(A statement of opinion; It is one person's opinion of what might happen in the future.)*

REVISIT THE BOOK

READER RESPONSE

1. Possible response for one statement: Fact: Mechanics check to make sure the airplane is safe to fly. Opinion: It is probably the most important step in preparing the airplane for its next flight. Opinion differs: There are many safety checks other than mechanical that are important.
2. Responses will vary.
3. Students should list unfamiliar words from the selection, look them up, and record the definitions. They should say whether they were able to guess the contextual meaning based on words or phrases in the paragraph.
4. Responses will vary.

EXTEND UNDERSTANDING Invite students to say which photos or maps interest them the most. Ask them to explain how these features add to their prior knowledge about the history of flight and airplane travel.

RESPONSE OPTIONS

WRITING Invite students to write about a time they flew on an airplane. Have them describe checking in at the airport, getting on the plane, the take-off, flight, landing, and getting their luggage. Students who have never flown can write a fictional account of a flight they would like to take. Encourage them to include their point of departure and their destination.

SOCIAL STUDIES CONNECTION

Time For
SOCIAL STUDIES

Students can find out more about the earliest flying machines or about the future of commercial space travel by visiting the library or using the Internet. Have them draw pictures of early airplanes or futuristic spacecraft. Have them label their pictures and exhibit them to the class.

Skill Work

TEACH/REVIEW VOCABULARY

Invite students to form two teams. Have one team read the definition of a vocabulary word and the other team to tell the word. Have teams reverse roles. Continue in a similar fashion with the remaining vocabulary words.

TARGET SKILL AND STRATEGY

FACT AND OPINION Tell students that a statement of *fact* can be proved true or false, while a statement of *opinion* is a statement of someone's judgment, belief, or way of thinking about something. Invite students, as they read, to look for statements of fact and statements of opinion. Then, have them cite personal activities (observing, weighing, measuring, and so on) they could use to verify whether the statements of fact are true or false. They may also cite references (encyclopedias and Internet sites).

PREDICT AND SET PURPOSE Explain that to *predict* means to tell what you think might happen next in a story or article based on what you have already read. Have students preview the headings and photographs. Based on their observations, have them make predictions about what they will be learning about in the text. Then have them set the purpose of reading to confirm or revise their predictions.

ADDITIONAL SKILL INSTRUCTION

SETTING Remind students that the setting is the time and place in which a story occurs. Explain that the book tells about a fictional family and their experiences traveling from Chicago to Denver in the present day—the 21st century. The story takes place in their home, in the airport, and in the airplane. That is the setting. Explain that the setting is important to this book because it deals with modern air-travel technology.

Name_____

Fact and Opinion

- A statement of **fact** is a statement that can be proved true or false.
- A statement of **opinion** tells someone's ideas, feelings, or beliefs. It cannot be proved true or false.

Directions Read the sentences below. On the line beside each sentence, write either *fact* or *opinion*. Give a reason for your response.

1. Charley Furnas, a mechanic by profession, was an airplane enthusiast who enjoyed helping the Wright brothers in his spare time.

_____

2. Being an airplane passenger has changed a lot over the nearly hundred years since Charley Furnas first flew.

_____

3. Perhaps the most exciting future possibility is that ordinary people will be able to fly in spacecraft.

_____

4. On Melville's first flight in SpaceShipOne, he left Earth's atmosphere and reached an altitude of 62 miles.

_____

5. The conveyor belt moves carry-on items through an x-ray machine that allows security personnel to see inside everything.

_____

6. Buying tickets online is better than buying them from a travel agent.

_____

7. People should not have to put up with the delays caused by security checks at airports.

_____

8. Much of the navigation of today's commercial jets is automated.

_____

9. When Grandma was a young woman, there were no movies, music, and telephones on airplanes.

_____

10. Air traffic control plays a crucial role in air travel.

_____

Vocabulary

Directions Choose the word from the box that best matches each definition.
Write the word on the line.

Check the Words You Know

___agent   ___altitude   ___confiscate   ___cruising

___kiosk   ___tarmac   ___taxis   ___turbulence

1. _____ small structure with wide open sides

2. _____ rough air encountered in flight

3. _____ a person who does business for someone else

4. _____ take away by force

Directions Write the word from the box that belongs in each group.

5. depth, height, _____

6. sidewalk, pavement, _____

7. traveling, driving, _____

8. steers, guides, _____

Directions Write a short paragraph on the future of commercial space flight. Use as many vocabulary
words as possible.

_____

_____

_____

_____

_____

_____

Unexpected Music

SUMMARY After reading *Unexpected Music*, students will not look at everyday objects the same way again. A wide variety of unusual instruments—spanning the ages and continents—are described. Even advanced readers will benefit from drawing on their prior knowledge of history and music to clarify the text.

LESSON VOCABULARY

aborigines	acoustic	antiquity
archaeologists	artifacts	oboe
ocarina	principles	reeds

INTRODUCE THE BOOK

INTRODUCE THE TITLE AND AUTHOR Discuss with students the title and author of *Unexpected Music*. Encourage students to comment on how the photograph on the cover relates to the title. Ask students how music can be unexpected.

BUILD BACKGROUND Have students create music with objects in the classroom. Students can tap on their desks, clap two coat hangers together, beat a ruler on a can or bottle, or blow through a drinking straw. Ask students how they might communicate with the sounds they make. Have them imagine what it might be like to communicate solely through music.

PREVIEW/USE TEXT FEATURES As students preview, have them count the number of different instruments named in the headings and shown in the illustrations and photographs. Draw students' attention to the household and natural objects mentioned in the text that may also be considered musical instruments.

READ THE BOOK

SET PURPOSE Encourage students to set a purpose for reading based on the sense they have developed of this reader by looking at the title, section headings, and illustrations.

STRATEGY SUPPORT: PRIOR KNOWLEDGE Remind students that although they are reading about unfamiliar instruments, they can use their *prior knowledge* of similar but familiar instruments to understand the text. Model how to make text-to-world connections when students come to page 17. On that page the author compares a glass armonica to running your wet finger around the edge of a glass. Ask students to share other places in the text where they can make connections between instruments in the text and their prior knowledge.

COMPREHENSION QUESTIONS

PAGES 3 AND 7 Which do you think came first—the bear bone flute or the didgeridoo? Why? *(Possible response: The bear bone flute came first because the Neanderthals who used it lived in prehistoric times. It is the earliest instrument discovered.)*

PAGE 15 What conclusion can you draw about the spoons being popular? *(They are commonly found items that anyone can play.)*

PAGE 16 Why are the glockenspiel, marimba, and xylophone all percussion instruments that can play melodies? *(These instruments have rows of bars that each play a different note when struck.)*

PAGE 16 What type of instrument is the gong? *(percussion)*

PAGE 21 What would you say is the main idea of this reader? *(Possible response: Over time, humans have used unusual and unexpected objects to make music.)*

REVISIT THE BOOK

READER RESPONSE

1. The first instruments discussed are wind instruments. *Wind*: flutes, horns, didgeridoo, pungi, bagpipes, pyrophone; *Percussion*: boulders, drums, o-daiko, gongs
2. Responses will vary but should include using students' understanding of wind and percussion instruments.
3. *Antiquity* deals with ancient times and *artifacts* are items made by humans.
4. Responses will vary.

EXTEND UNDERSTANDING Pause when students finish reading page 11 and then have students look at the percussion instruments on page 10. Encourage students to predict how the instruments are played and why they are considered percussion instruments.

RESPONSE OPTIONS

WRITING Have students imagine a new instrument. Invite them to both draw and write about their idea.

SOCIAL STUDIES CONNECTION

Time For SOCIAL STUDIES

Have students plot the instruments discussed in the book on a map of the world. Invite them to find out about even more instruments on the Internet or at a library and add them to the map.

Skill Work

TEACH/REVIEW VOCABULARY

Have students practice using context clues to find the meaning of vocabulary words. Begin with the word *archaeologists* on page 3. Invite students to say the meaning in their own words and explain which context clues helped them understand the word. Repeat for each vocabulary word.

ELL Write the vocabulary words on separate index cards as well as any additional words you think will be difficult for English language learners. Hold up a card and help students define it by using it in sentences and having students use context clues to determine meaning.

TARGET SKILL AND STRATEGY

SEQUENCE Point out that a time line is an excellent way to show *sequence*. Ask students to plot the evolution of music and musical instruments on a time line. Lead students to organize the time line by general time periods, such as Prehistoric, Ancient, and Modern, instead of specific dates.

PRIOR KNOWLEDGE Activating *prior knowledge* will aid students' comprehension of the evolution of music. Review with students the three types of connections they can make: text-to-self—the feeling of hearing or playing an instrument, text-to-world—general knowledge of music and instruments, text-to-text—books about music or history. Have students note that many of the unusual instruments discussed in this reader are likened to instruments students are likely to know, and this helps students develop a concept of the unfamiliar instrument.

ADDITIONAL SKILL INSTRUCTION

DRAW CONCLUSIONS Remind students that a *conclusion* is a sensible decision reached after thinking about details and facts in the text. When drawing a conclusion, readers often use prior knowledge. Have students pause at the end of each section and write down one conclusion they can draw. After reading, prompt students to share and explain their conclusions from the text.

Sequence

- **Sequence** refers to the order of events in both fiction and nonfiction.
- Sequence can also refer to the steps in a process.

Directions Write a summary of *Unexpected Music*. Include at least three of the facts listed below. Organize the facts in sequence. Use time order cues such as dates and time periods, and/or time order words such as *first, then, following,* and *recently.*

- The didgeridoo is an ancient instrument made by Australian aborigines. It could be 40,000 years old.
- Bagpipes were played by the ancient cultures of Greece and Rome.
- Stone Age percussion instruments were found in India.

- The first pyrophones were built in the 1700s and 1800s.
- The earliest instrument known is a flute made from a bone of a bear at least 43,000 years ago.
- Spoons and saws were popular instruments of the early 1900s in the United States.

_____

_____

_____

_____

_____

_____

_____

_____

_____

_____

_____

_____

_____

Name_____

Vocabulary

Directions Choose the word from the box that best matches each definition.
Write the word on the line.

Check the Words You Know

___aborigines   ___acoustic   ___antiquity   ___archaeologists   ___artifacts

___oboe   ___ocarina   ___principles   ___reeds

---

1. _____ scientists who study the people, customs, and life of ancient times

2. _____ basic rules of science that explain how something works

3. _____ anything made by human skill or work

4. _____ thin pieces of wood, metal, or plastic inside some musical instruments that produce a sound when a current of air moves them

5. _____ a small wind instrument, traditionally made of clay, with finger holes and a whistlelike mouthpiece

Directions Draw a line to match the synonyms.

6. aborigines   reed instrument

7. oboe   not amplified

8. antiquity   natives

9. acoustic   ancient times

Directions Write a short paragraph about one of the instruments from *Unexpected Music*.
Use as many vocabulary words as possible.

_____

_____

_____

_____

_____

Story Prediction from Previewing

Title _____

Read the title and look at the pictures in the story.
What do you think a problem in the story might be?

I think a problem might be _____

_____

_____

After reading _____,
draw a picture of one of the problems in the story.

Story Prediction from Vocabulary

Title _____

Look at the title above and the list of words and phrases below.
Write sentences that predict who and what this story might be about.

> **Words and Phrases**

Characters: _____

_____

Problem: _____

_____

_____

_____

Events: _____

_____

_____

Outcome: _____

_____

_____

_____

KWL Chart

Topic _____

What We **K** now	What We **W** ant to Know	What We **L** earned

Vocabulary Frame

Word

Association or Symbol

Predicted definition:

_____

_____

One good sentence:

_____

_____

_____

Verified definition:

_____

_____

Another good sentence:

_____

_____

_____

Story Sequence A

Title _____

Beginning

Middle

End

Story Sequence B

Title _____

Characters

Setting

Problem

Events

_____

_____

_____

_____

_____

_____

_____

_____

Solution

Story Elements

Title _____

This story is about _____

_____
(name the characters)

This story takes place _____

_____
(where and when)

The action begins when _____

_____

_____

Then, _____

_____

_____

Next, _____

_____

_____

After that, _____

_____

_____

The story ends when _____

_____

_____

Theme: _____

_____

Question the Author

Title _____

Author _____ **Page** _____

1. What does the author tell you?	
2. Why do you think the author tells you that?	
3. Does the author say it clearly?	
4. What would make it clearer?	
5. How would you say it instead?	

Plot Structure

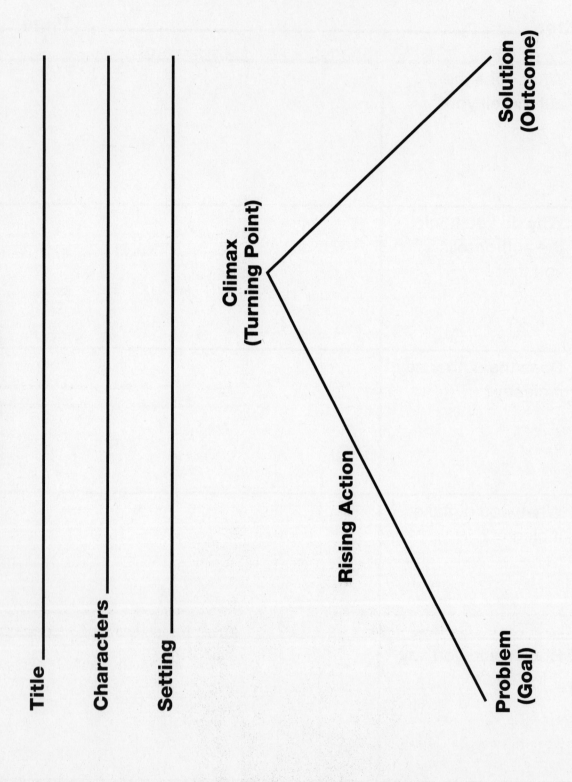

Title

Characters

Setting

Problem
(Goal)

Rising Action

Climax
(Turning Point)

Solution
(Outcome)

Story Comparison

Title A _____ | **Title B** _____

Characters	Characters

Setting	Setting

Events	Events

Ending	Ending

Web

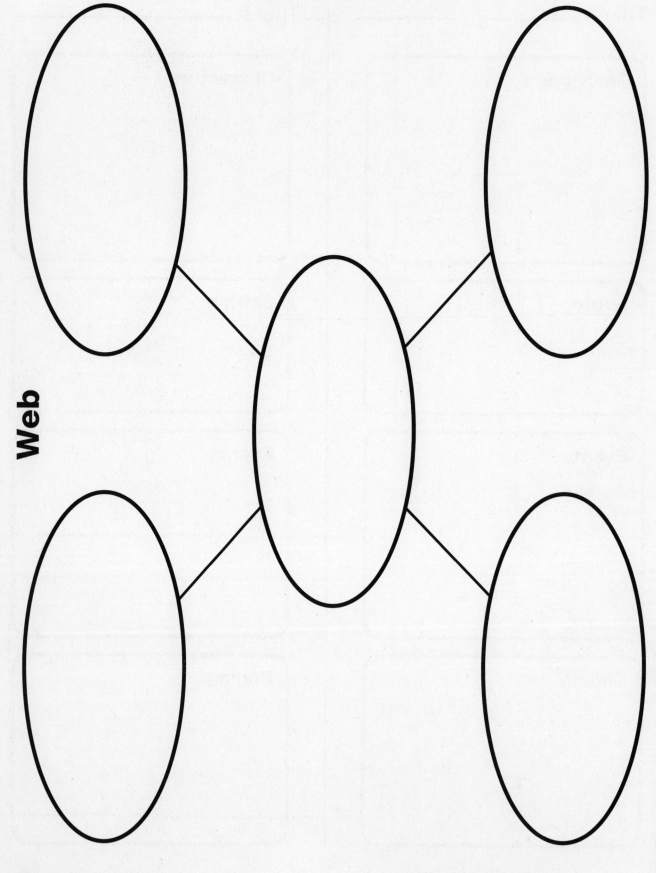

Main Idea

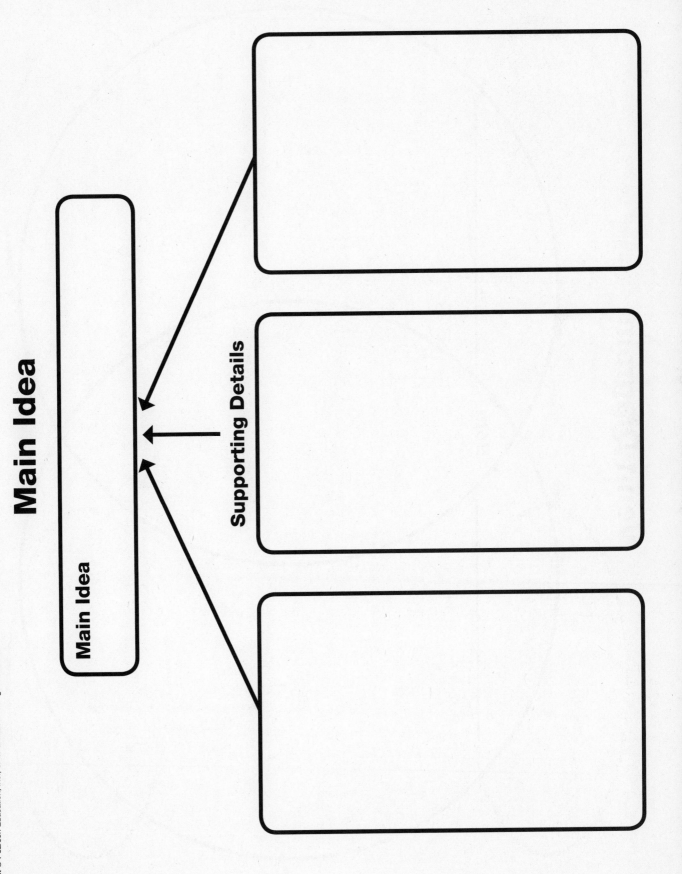

Main Idea

Supporting Details

Venn Diagram

Both

Compare and Contrast

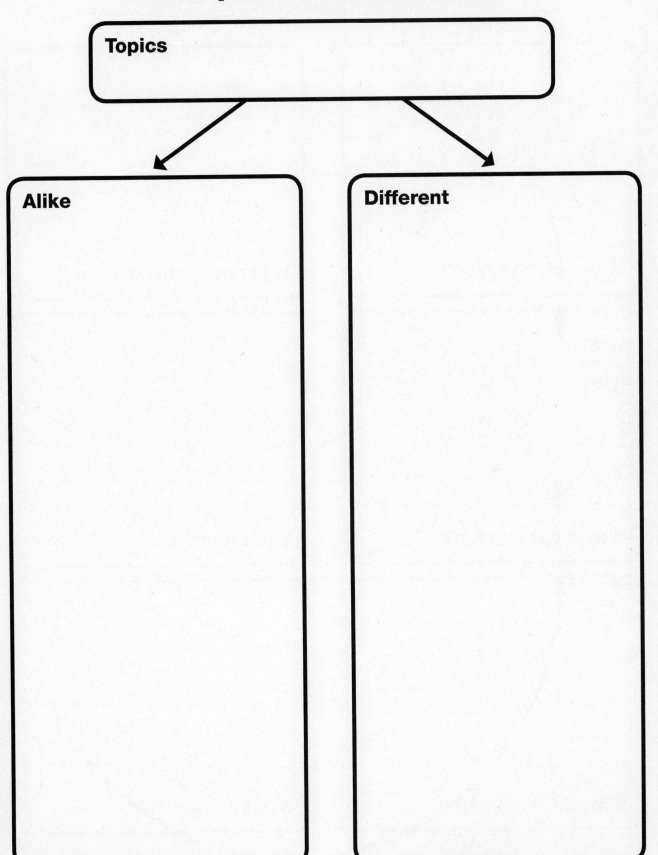

Topics

Alike

Different

Cause and Effect

Causes   **Effects**

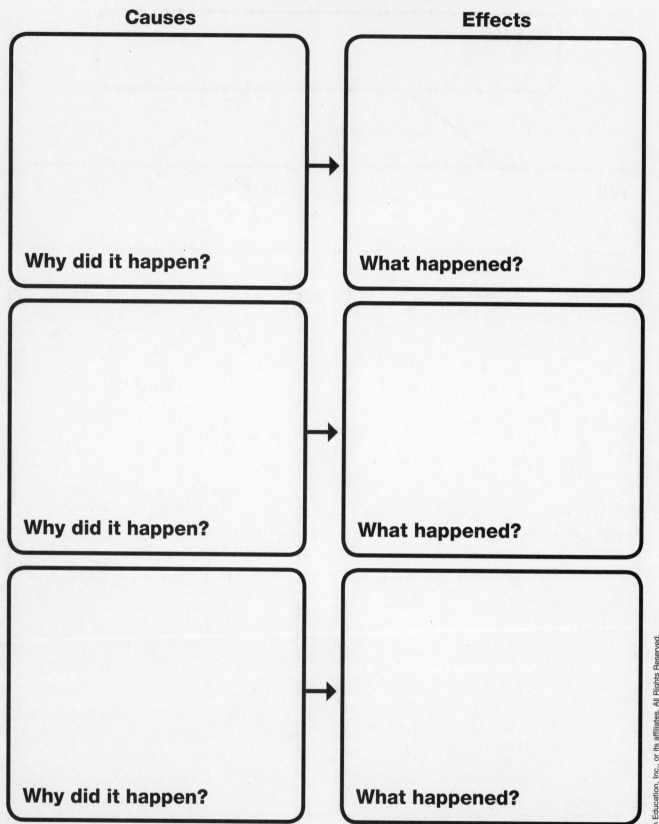

Why did it happen?   What happened?

Why did it happen?   What happened?

Why did it happen?   What happened?

Problem and Solution

Problem

↓

Attempts to Solve the Problem

↓

Solution

Time Line

Date ____

Steps in a Process

Process _____

Step 1

↓

Step 2

↓

Step 3

↓

Step 4

↓

Step 5

Three-Column Chart

Four-Column Chart

Five-Column Chart

Five-Column Chart

Answer Key

Leveled Reader Practice Pages

The Signs p. 14
🎯 **CHARACTER AND PLOT**
TITLE: The Signs
CHARACTERS: Nathan, Nathan's mother, Nathan's grandfather
SETTING: The Gila River Indian Community in Arizona. Most of the story takes place during a walk in the Sacaton Mountains.
PROBLEM: Nathan must decide whether he would like to move with his mother to Gila River. During a walk with his grandfather, Grandfather becomes ill and Nathan runs for help.
EVENTS: Nathan and his grandfather take a hike in the mountains. Nathan thinks about what to tell his mother about the move. Grandfather becomes sick on the hike. Nathan runs for help. Grandfather tells Nathan to take the shortcut, but Nathan isn't sure he knows how to get back. Nathan decides to trust his instincts and finds help for Grandfather.
FORESHADOWING: On page 5, Nathan remembers being with his mother and grandfather near a butte in the desert when he was younger.
SOLUTION: Nathan is finally able to get Grandfather the help he needs. Nathan now knows what his decision about the move will be.

The Signs p. 15 Vocabulary
1. d   4. g   7. i
2. f   5. h   8. e
3. a   6. b   9. c
10–12.   Sentences will vary.

Weather Forecasting p. 18
🎯 **CAUSE AND EFFECT**
Possible responses given.
1. Warm humid air rises, and then cools. Winds collide and push warm, moist air upward.
2. high winds; flooding caused by coastal storm surge
3. loss of life
4. damages of residences and businesses
5. Responses will vary

Weather Forecasting p. 19 Vocabulary
1. radiosondes   7. troposphere
2. Doppler radar   8. meteorologists
3. barometer   9. troposphere
4. anemometer   10. atmosphere
5. hygrometer   11–12. Sentences will vary.
6. weather forecasts

The Medicine Harvest p. 22
🎯 **SETTING AND THEME**
Possible responses given.
1. the wild California coast that is nature's pharmacy of flowers, roots, and leaves
2. Red Hawk is learning from his grandfather about the different healing plants.
3. Yes. The setting is a place where Native Americans lived and where there were many plants.

The Medicine Harvest p. 23 Vocabulary
1. purify
2. urgency
3. cultivated
4. quell
5. ominous
6. idly
7–10. Sentences will vary.

The Journey of African American Athletes p. 26
🎯 **FACT AND OPINION**
Statements of Fact: Exclusion from sports was not the only challenge African American athletes faced. Many were called rude names and threatened in person, by phone, and by mail. But Tiger Woods has not faced as many obstacles as earlier African American athletes. By the time he was two, he was hitting golf balls.
Statements of Opinion: From an early age, Tiger displayed great athletic skill. Tiger has achieved some amazing records. But perhaps what is most impressive about his golf career is this: Although there have been African American golf champions in the past, Woods remains the only African American golfer who regularly competes in professional golf tournaments.

The Journey of African American Athletes p. 27 Vocabulary
1. adversity—condition of misfortune or distress
2. amateur—someone who plays something for pleasure, instead of for money or as a profession
3. taunts—jeers; mocking or insulting remarks
4. discrimination—act of showing an unfair difference in treatment
5. inferior—below most others; low in quality
6. integrated—when a public place or group has been opened to all races
7. prejudiced—having an unreasonable dislike for someone or something
8. prohibited—forbidden by law from doing something
9–12.   Sentences will vary.

The Land of Opportunity p. 30
CAUSE AND EFFECT
1. They were poor and wanted a better life in America.
2. overcrowding
3. They were determined to provide a better life for their families.
4. Immigrants helped other immigrants from their homeland, sharing their resources.
5. They were disappointed, sad.
6. cause
7. effect
8. effect
9. cause
10. cause

The Land of Opportunity p. 31 Vocabulary
1. steerage
2. citizens
3. emigrate
4. tenement
5. interpreter
6. detainees
7. naturalized
8. barracks
9–10. Sentences will vary.

Our Essential Oceans p. 34
COMPARE AND CONTRAST
1. Possible response: Aquaculture is fish farming in the oceans. Agriculture is farming on land.
2. China is known for seaweed and carp. Japan is known for many varieties of fish and shellfish and seaweed. Russia is known for sturgeon for its caviar. Europe is known for eels. North America is known for trout, catfish, salmon, shrimp, and oysters.
3. Possible response: Hydroelectic plants house huge turbines that use rushing water from the ocean to generate electricity. That is different from solar energy, which comes from the sun.
4. Some environmental and wildlife protection groups fear that the ocean wind farms might harm migrating birds or hurt the fishing industry.
5. Some people prefer the more leisurely trip that an ocean liner provides. It reminds them of times past.

Our Essential Oceans p. 34 Vocabulary
1. shellfish
2. tumors
3. atmosphere
4. turbines
5. ecosystems
6. distill
Paragraphs will vary.

The Most Dangerous Woman in America p. 38
SEQUENCE
Possible responses:
1. It describes her appearance at a demonstration that was later known as the children's march, held to protest child labor practices.
2. The events in italics describe one key event near the end of Mary Jones' life. Moving back and forth in time between this event and her past helps show that the children's march is a sum of her experiences and background.
3. illness of her husband and children; losing everything in the fire

The Most Dangerous Woman in America
p. 39 Vocabulary
Adjective: deplorable, humane, lavish, oppressive, regulated, resolute, staunch
Noun: famine
Adverb: indefinitely
Verb: lavish, regulated, staunch
1–4. Sentences will vary.

Moving to Mali p. 42
COMPARE AND CONTRAST
1–2. Both are ambitious; both like to improve things; both like working with chickens and agriculture. Georgia wants to improve things in a place that needs it more than where she lives.
3. Unlike her home in Maine, Georgia's home in Mali is made out of mud, is very small, and has no electricity.
4–5. When they bought it, the garden center had been a tumbledown place with a sagging greenhouse and a barn with a hole in the roof. Now, customers come from all over to buy their flowers.
6–7. Both are go-getters; both have big plans. Moussa is Muslim; Georgia is not.
8. Both are the same age; both notice things around them.

Moving to Mali p. 43 Vocabulary
1. rummaging
2. simplicity
3. efficiency
4. ambition
5. thriving
6. volunteer
7. moped
8. volunteer
9. waste
10. selling
11. moped
12. simplicity
13. laziness
14. failing

The Talker p. 46
AUTHOR'S PURPOSE
Possible responses given
1. inform readers about the role of Navajo code talkers in World War II.
2. including numerous details about the lives and work of fictional code talkers.
3. entertain readers with a moving story about a man's struggle to do the right thing, even though it was difficult.
4. making Joe a sympathetic character who is poorly treated by others, yet does his job the best he can.
5. show that the code talkers were not respected even though they performed an important role.

The Talker p. 47 Vocabulary
Possible responses:
ACROSS
1. limits
2. people trained to use Navajo words as code to send secret messages.
3. a subdivision of a battalion; a unit of soldiers
4. large military units of three or more companies or other smaller subunits
5. exchange of thoughts and messages
6. fortress
7. the act of signing up people to be in the armed forces
DOWN
1. appreciation of an achievement
8. related to the armed forces
9. take a code apart to understand it

The National Guard: Today's Minutemen p. 50
AUTHOR'S PURPOSE
Possible responses:
Author's Purpose: to inform
Supporting Details: The author gives the history behind the National Guard; the author discusses Civil Rights protections; the author discusses international defense

The National Guard: Today's Minutemen
p. 51 Vocabulary
Nouns: citizen-soldiers, National Guard, relief, riot, steed, troops, volunteers
Verbs: defending, mobilize (also accept riot)
Possible responses:
1. *Citizen-soldiers* were often farmers who fought during wartime.
2. The soldiers were responsible for *defending* the fort.
3. It was time to *mobilize* the troops to fight.
4. The *National Guard* has been serving the nation for many years.
5. The end of the battle brought *relief* to the soldiers' families.
6. The crowd pushed so that police feared a *riot*.
7. The Minuteman jumped upon his *steed* to ride to war.
8. Thousands of *troops* were sent abroad to fight the war.
9. I needed several *volunteers* to help with this charity.

Philo and His Invention p. 54
SEQUENCE OF EVENTS
1. In a flash he realized how to make television work!
2. In his lab, he successfully demonstrated the transmission of an electronic image to a receiver, or television screen.
3. Vladimir Zworykin showed up at Philo's lab.
4. RCA had taken Philo to court over patent issues.
5. A statue of Philo is added to the National Statuary Hall in Washington, D.C.

Philo and His Invention
p. 55 Vocabulary
1. nemesis
2. scrutiny
3. manifests
4. envisioned
5. mechanics
6. furrows
7. technology
8. quest
9. funding
10–13. Sentences will vary.

Art's Inspiration p. 58
MAIN IDEA AND DETAILS
Possible responses given.
1. Borrowing designs from other artists was common and considered a compliment at that time.
2. Artists have always studied the art of earlier times.
3. Copying showed respect and admiration for older artists.
4. Copying contributed to the preservation of past artistic styles.

Art's Inspiration p. 59
1. incorporated
2–3. Baroque; sinuous
4. cast
5–6. intricate; facade
7. cubism
8–9. innovative, razing
Paragraphs will vary.

What's New with Dinosaur Fossils? p. 62
FACT AND OPINION
1. opinion
2. fact
3. fact
4. opinion
5. fact
6. fact
7. opinion
8. Responses will vary.
9. Responses will vary.

What's New with Dinosaur Fossils?
p. 63 Vocabulary
1. herbivorous
2. trackways
3. collaborator
4. vertebrae
5. theropods
6. olfactory bulbs
7. avid
8. descendants
9. carnivorous
10–11. consensus, contention

The Blues Evolution p. 66
MAIN IDEA AND DETAILS
Main idea: Blues music has influenced other types of music.
Supporting Details: Pop music owes much of its emotional singing to blues greats such as B.B. King. Jazz music has borrowed heavily from the blues over the years.

The Blues Evolution p. 67 Vocabulary
1. reggae
2. inception
3. prodigy
4. spawned
5. yodeling
6. rhythm and blues
7. coalesced
8. mentors
9. genre
10–12. Sentences will vary.

Hollywood Special Effects p. 70
GRAPHIC SOURCES
1. a poster
2–3. The poster is designed to interest moviegoers in seeing the movie *It*, which starred the actress Clara Bow.
4. Both are movie posters, but the one on page 11 shows the special effects makeup that is part of the movie *Frankenstein*.
5. The author may have wanted to show that special effects could create seemingly everyday events.
6–7. It shows how a moviemaker used a split screen to create the illusion of twins. It shows what the author is describing in the text.
8–9. a cover from *Time* magazine; that special effects, and especially those of George Lucas, were getting national attention.
10. Possible response: Special effects are very important in making movies.

Hollywood Special Effects p. 71 Vocabulary
1. continuous motion
2. optical illusion
3. cinema
4. sensors
5. blue screen
6. matte painting
7. technology

Possible responses:
8. We were amazed by the optical illusion that the actor was just floating in mid-air.
9. The advances in technology in the past decade are amazing.
10. Jennifer called to see if I might like to go with her to the cinema.

Cheaper, Faster, and Better p. 74
DRAW CONCLUSIONS
Possible responses:
1. Resources, such as going to the library or needing an encyclopedia or using white out for mistakes were available but getting to them or using them was
difficult and time consuming.
2. Students had to go to libraries to use reference books and had to use manual typewriters.
3. Shopping took more time and work, too.
4. People went to malls or shopping centers or pored over catalogues.
5. Possible response: Technology would have made shopping, studying, and selecting movies more convenient and less expensive activities.

Cheaper, Faster, and Better p. 75 Vocabulary
1. telecommuting
2. computer viruses
3. World Wide Web
4. CD-ROM
5. Industrial Revolution
6. search engine
7. e-mail
8. Internet
9. Computer Age
10. word processors

Operation Inspiration p. 78
GENERALIZE
1. valid; Stephen Marino, Representative Ari Poth, Senator Nan Rich
2. faulty; a child dies from malaria every 30 seconds
3. faulty; Her friends were not supportive, and some even laughed at her efforts.
4. valid; By fall of 2005, Daniel had more than 10,000 requests for computer training.
5. faulty; Jack and his dad, Katherine and her mom, Chanelle, David

Operation Inspiration p. 79
1. ally
2. vulnerable
3. discourage
4. sponsors
5. resources
6. liabilities
7. Documentary
8. Legislation
9. Daunting
10–12. Sentences will vary.

Can Humans Make a Home in Outer Space? p. 82
GRAPHIC SOURCES
Earth to moon: 238,855 miles
Earth to Mars: 48,769,273 miles
Possible response: Must learn to live in zero gravity; on long space flight, would need to spend a lot of time exercising to decrease effects of zero gravity; could possibly use centripetal force instead of gravity on space station; could have orbiting space colony with vegetation to supply oxygen and food; could create solar power plants in space; space travel is expensive.
Possible responses for additional questions: Will an asteroid hit Earth? Will space travel save us? How can experiments in low gravity labs produce advances in medicine and technology?

Can Humans Make a Home in Outer Space?
p. 83 Vocabulary
1. deflect
2. contend
3. asteroids
4. astronomically
5. cycle
6. extraterrestrial
7. vegetation

Nathaniel Comes to Town p. 86
GENERALIZE
Possible responses:
1. Nathaniel will want to make new friends.
2. Nathaniel will need to find his way to his new class.
3. Nathaniel will want to learn about school sports.
4. Nathaniel will want to make Drew his best friend.
5. All new students have to make new friends at a new school and fit in with the other students.
6. It could be difficult for an older student to be friends with a younger student.
7. It could be difficult to eat lunch with students from your own class.
8. It is difficult to fit in with an existing group.
9. It is difficult to find your way around the school.
10. It is difficult to find a new best firend.

Nathaniel Comes to Town p. 87 Vocabulary
1. foreboding
2. gallantly
3. humiliation
4. jostling
5. annoyingly
6. skeptically

Paragraphs will vary.

What Makes Great Athletes? p. 90
DRAW CONCLUSIONS
Possible responses given.
1. because the games were held in honor of Zeus
2. because Zeus was the most powerful of the Greek gods
3. our interest and knowledge of sporting events come from ancient Greece
4. yes, because scholars think so
5. Responses will vary.

What Makes Great Athletes? p. 91 Vocabulary
1. Colosseum
2. persistence
3. mastery
4. artifacts
5. endurance
6. esteem
7. archaeologists
8. coordination
9. rigorous

The Sandwich Brigade p. 94
PLOT AND CHARACTER
Possible responses:
Title: The Sandwich Brigade
Main Characters: Herb, Bob, Pete
Setting: Benderville, small town in upstate NY
Problem: Herb, Bob, and Pete are retired and bored.
Plot: Herb, Bob, and Pete try out a number of different activities (karate class, pottery class, book club).
Solution: They start a service to deliver food to the elderly people who can't get out and enlist others to help them.

The Sandwich Brigade p. 95 Vocabulary
1. retirement
2. putter
3. pondered
4. recruit
5. retirement
6. pondered
7. putter
8. recruit
9. pondered
10. retirement

Space Travel Inventions p. 98
GRAPHIC SOURCES
Possible responses:
1. The Telstar 1 transmitted between England and Andover, Maine and Washington, D.C.
2. The dome shape allows light in plus rain runs off the roof which dries quickly.
3. The caption compares how a digital image processor can be used in space for taking computerized moon pictures and in hospitals for showing organs. The photograph allows us to see how the invention is used in a hospital.
4. It allows me to see how difficult a Dead Sea Scroll would be to read without technology.

Space Travel Inventions p. 99 Vocabulary
1. friction
2. transmitter
3. absorb
4. shuttle
5. impacts
6. relics
7. perilous
8. insulation

Paragraphs will vary.

Astronauts and Cosmonauts p. 102
AUTHOR'S PURPOSE
Possible responses:
1. to express
2. expresses the wonder people have always had about beauty and mystery of stars
3. to inform
4. gives information about beginning of space race
5. expresses people's feelings about space and draws readers into the topic to inform them

Astronauts and Cosmonauts p. 103 Vocabulary
1. rendezvous
2. gravity
3. strenuous
4. beleaguered
5. simulator
6. germinate
7. aerospace
8. capsule
9. dissolved

Sentences will vary.

The Shaping on Continents p. 106
CAUSE AND EFFECT
1. Pangaea broke into two distinct landmasses.
2. Earth's one great ocean separated into smaller oceans.
3. Scientists developed the theory of plate tectonics.
4. Molten rock from within the mantle spews forth, creating new ocean floor.
5. Very deep trenches occur.
6. The ocean floor slides under the land.
7. The landmasses fold and crumple, producing mountain ranges.
8. An earthquake occurs.
9. The volcano erupts.
10. We are not likely to see much change in Earth during our lifetimes.

The Shaping of Continents p. 107 Vocabulary
1. subduction
2. magma
3. diverge
4. unconventional
5. fossils

Answers will vary but should include the words *plastic*, *converge*, and *supercontinent*.

From Territory to Statehood p. 110
GENERALIZE
1. valid
2. valid
3. faulty
4. faulty
5. valid
6. faulty
7. faulty
8. valid
9–10. Responses will vary.

From Territory to Statehood p. 111 Vocabulary
1. inhabited
2. ratification
3. expedition
4. annexed
5. compromise
6. precedent
7. bill
8. interpreter
9. inhabited
10. compromise
11. annexed

How the Wolves Saved Yellowstone p. 114
DRAW CONCLUSIONS
Possible responses:
1. Renee Askins was an important person in ensuring that the plan succeeded.
2. She helped the government by educating the ranchers about the importance of wolves balancing the ecosystem.
3. The ranchers were satisfied and willing to accept the plan.
4. they would be reimbursed for loss of livestock due to wolves; they were allowed to kill a wolf that attacked their livestock

How the Wolves Saved Yellowstone p. 115
Vocabulary
1. rigidly, obstinately
2. theatrical, emotional
3. searches, grazers
4. conference, powwow
5. storing, stashing
6. reasonable, valid
7. scale, limit
8. refund, repay
9. unyielding, determinedly
10. extraordinary ability; unusual skill

Mixed-Up Vegetables p. 118
MAIN IDEA AND DETAILS
Possible responses:
Main Idea: Transgenic vegetables have benefits and risks.
Supporting Details: Vegetables taste better; Vegetables can be healthier; Vegetables can resist pesticides; Vegetables can endanger wildlife.
Main Idea: Many vegetables are altered to improve them.
Supporting Details: Cabbage and potato resist pests better; Broccoli, celery gain improved taste; Soybeans increase nutritional value; Cucumbers and artichokes are more disease resistant.

Mixed-Up Vegetables p. 119 Vocabulary
1. pesticides
2. transgenic organism
3. gene
4. beneficial
5. genetically altered
Paragraphs will vary.

Precious Goods: From Salt to Silk p. 122
COMPARE AND CONTRAST
Alike: rich traders, important trade routes opened, cultural exchange, military invasion and conflict
Different: China guarded secret to making silk. California acquired statehood. Diamonds and oil have led to military conflicts or to help pay for wars.

Precious Goods: From Salt to Silk p. 123
1. malleable
2. commodities
3. luster
4. molten
5. excavating
6. synthetic
7. microorganisms
8. preserve
Paragraphs will vary.

Traveling by Plane p. 126
FACT AND OPINION
1. fact: can be proved true or false
2. fact: can be proved true or false
3. opinion: statement of someone's beliefs/cannot be proved
4. fact: can be proved true or false
5. fact: can be proved true or false
6. opinion: statement of someone's beliefs/cannot be proved
7. opinion: statement of someone's beliefs/cannot be proved
8. fact: can be proved true or false
9. fact: can be proved true or false
10. fact: can be proved true or false

Traveling by Plane p. 127 Vocabulary
1. kiosk
2. turbulence
3. agent
4. confiscate
5. altitude
6. tarmac
7. cruising
8. taxis
Paragraphs will vary.

Unexpected Music p. 130
SEQUENCE
Possible response: Throughout history music has been created in unexpected ways. First the earliest instrument known is a flute made from a bone of a bear at least 43,000 years ago. The didgeridoo is an ancient instrument made by Australian aborigines. It could be 40,000 years old. Stone Age percussion instruments were found in India. More recently spoons and saws were popular instruments of the early 1900s in the United States.

Unexpected Music p. 131 Vocabulary
1. archaeologists
2. principles
3. artifacts
4. reeds
5. ocarina
6. natives
7. reed instrument
8. ancient times
9. not amplified
Paragraphs will vary.